McGregor Says

The Seasons
Go Around and Around

McGregor Says

The Seasons
Go Around and Around

Jim McGregor

ISBN: 978-0-9738783-3-2
ISBN Digital: 978-0-9738783-4-9

This collection of stories is dedicated to Shirley who encourages me, inspires me, and brings the sunshine to every season of my life.

Foreword

For many years I had the opportunity to talk to the public from these pages—usually reporting on emergencies or disasters or bringing a message of awareness or prevention.

My Dad would read these weekly reports, put the paper down and say: "It always reads 'McGregor says,' when is it going to tell me 'McGregor does'?"

Now I have been given the exciting opportunity to share some time with you each week, usually on a lighter, more upbeat note. I believe that when someone is given a chance to speak or write that they should make the best of it, educate, entertain, enlighten.

This is the second collection of my columns, the first one titled, "McGregor Says Special Days Make Lasting Memories." This collection of stories is about the seasons. Not just the four natural seasons we all experience but the also the seasons of our lives that change dramatically as we grow, age and experience new life or grieve as a life passes.

My hometown of Langley, British Columbia, Canada is approximately 100 km east of Vancouver and tucked in between the Coast Mountains to the north and the Pacific Ocean about twenty minutes away to the south. Geographically this means that if you don't like the current weather, wait twenty minutes as a hot sunny day can be interrupted by some thunderclouds, hail and rain and back to sun again in less than an hour.

Tourists often speak of our four distinct seasons: freezing rain, steady rain, warm rain and cold rain. But if you have spent any time here you will enjoy apple, cheery and lilac blossoms in the spring, turning to leaves painted with every shade of red orange and brown in the fall. You will bake in the summer sunshine and wake to a calendar picture of pure white snow draped over branches and blanketing the ground backed by a bright blue sky.

I was given the honour of writing the lyrics for a song for Langley City's 50th birthday. I gave the words to Peter Luongo, the Director of the world famous Langley Ukulele Ensemble and we produced the song, "Langley City -The Place to Be."

As you read the stories I hope you will remember the stories and seasons of your life as it has moved from time to time and place to place to bring you where you are now.

These stories have been written over a twelve-year period and it is interesting to see some of the phrases, technology or references to events has changed over that period of time. The reader may notice some repetition of phrases or thoughts and that just means they are important to me, and a reflection of how I approach life or celebrate family.

I would be most pleased to come to your home and find my book on your coffee table with a page corner turned down to mark your place or water marks on the cover because you left it on the patio table on your deck. Or better yet find the bottom of the pages wrinkled because you dozed off reading it in the tub.

I hope to see you enjoy the stories, because as the song says, "Without an audience, there ain't no show!" Besides, it's healthy to sit and take a break once in a while. At least, that's what McGregor says.

Langley City "The Place to Be"

Have you walked the nature trails in spring
And seen summer growing there,
Smelled the perfumed breeze
From the blossomed trees
And breathed the clean fresh air?

Have you ever sat up on Murrayville Hill
On a warm clear summer night?
And watched the City below
Set the valley aglow
With a blanket of twinkling light?

Then and Now, from field and farm,
Then and Now, A City full of charm,
Chorus:
Every Smile, every face,
That we see in this place
Shouts out proud to you and me,
Langley City is the Place to Be!

Have you ever walked along Michaud
On a late fall afternoon
When the maples there
Make you quite aware
The season's changing soon?

Have you walked downtown on a winter night
To catch the Christmas show,
When those sidewalk trees
With their electric leaves
Casting shadows across the snow?

Then and Now, from field and farm,
Then and Now, A City full of charm,
Every Smile, every face,
That we see in this place
Shouts out proud to you and me,
Langley City is the Place to Be!

Then and Now, from field and farm,
Then and Now, A City full of charm,
Every Smile, every face,
That we see in this place
Shouts out proud to you and me,
Langley City is the Place to B

SPRING

Spring

There are lots of things happening this weekend as we approach the vernal equinox, the first day of spring, followed by Good Friday and Easter. The almanac tells us this is the earliest Easter has arrived since 1913 and it won't be this early again for over 200 years. It seems that in western cultures, the Easter dates are based on a lunar calendar very similar to the Hebrew calendar and way back in 325 AD they started to set the Easter dates based on the first Ecclesiastical full moon after March 20th. Does that clear it up for you?

I wonder if anyone has told Mother Nature about this sophisticated arrangement. She is probably just as busy as any other mother and I'm sure she would be more than happy to have it set on the same weekend every year. After all, March is a very tricky weather month and while she is popping up daffodils in Vancouver she is still dumping snow back east and moving the Easter days around each year is no doubt a very real source of irritation to her. That may explain her unpredictability this month.

But it doesn't matter what we say or do or how we determine the comings and goings of the seasons because their changes are constant and controlled by forces that do not have the constraints of calendars or clocks. We however, need to have some sense that we are in control. We move our clocks ahead and back to suit our needs or we add a day once every four years or maybe we have a summit meeting and adjust the atomic clock. But the tides come and go, the sun rises and sets and the moon waxes and wanes over us the same as it did for the cavemen.

I think we should spend less time trying to change the universe and more time trying to enjoy what it brings us each day. At least that's what McGregor says.

Born Again

Sometime in the late fall,
We shed our gay summer blooms
And begin to prepare
For the dormancy ahead;
Gathering protective cover around us,
We instinctively prepare
For the onslaught of winter
And the trials it brings;
We burrow into layers,
We seek the peace of darkness
And the silence of hibernation;
We wait.
Sometime, as the days lengthen,
We stir and cast our eyes to the sky;
The breeze carries promise,
The sharp edge of the day has softened,
One layer is peeled away in anticipation;
We instinctively stretch,
We re-establish our roots,
We are pulled upward by the warmth.
Sometime in early March,
We break into the light;
We feel the sun's energy flow through our veins
And we expose ourselves to the world
We have survived.
We instinctively begin the cycle once again

Jim McGregor

We breathe in the spring air,
We begin to plan, to grow;
We arrogantly believe that
We are the authors of our winter survival,
We only have to look around,
The snow drop here, the crocus there
The bud on the fruit tree and the blade of grass,
Our spring,
No more a spectacular achievement
Than the very least of these.

Where City and Country Meet

Warning! This column is about manure. I'll pause while my brother says, "So far they've all been manure!" I have noticed some of the local farmers getting ready to spread their fields. This will bring about some calls to the City and Township switchboards asking what that smell is and demanding something be done about it. The receptionists will be tactful and diplomatic, all the time wanting to shout, "Hey, you live in Langley."

I grew up with many dairy farmers and they will tell you that smell is the smell of money. It turns brown fields green, fills silos and hay lofts, and is an important part of the cycle that puts milk on your cereal and cream in your coffee. It won't kill you.

In my old tire shop days, us service guys would get the dreaded call to head out to a farm to fix a flat on a 'honey wagon.' Now a honey wagon was a large tank designed to spread liquid manure. It's pulled across the field on truck rims modified to hold surplus aircraft tires. You would drive the service truck across the partially spread field, crawl under the tank and place the jacks, then manhandle the tire off the rim. Of course, everything was covered with 'honey.' My uncle used to say, 'What doesn't kill you, makes you stronger.' Well, you were certainly 'stronger' when you got back to the shop.

The only thing that made the trip worthwhile was when the farmer brought out a glass of tart lemonade, or dipped some ice-cold milk out of the dairy tank or, shared a pull off some homemade wine tucked between the hay bales.

Now, we have more challenges with long term composting and open pits and they are being addressed. I suggest that our local Development Services departments have at least one person on staff that has a farming background. Someone whose PHD means they can Pile it Higher, Deeper than anyone else! They would be responsible to liaise with developers and realtors and explain this annual olfactory assault so that it doesn't come as a surprise to the new condo purchaser. Something as simple as asking, "Are you aware that cows and horses will be co-habitating in your neighbourhood?"

I don't have much patience for people who "move to the country" and then complain about barking dogs, ice cream truck music, noisy kids in cul-de-sacs, or country smells.

If you buy a house next to a soccer field, kids might just come there to play soccer, don't complain to City hall about it.

I'm sure there are some pretty bad odours and disturbing sounds in downtown Kandahar but I wouldn't trade them. I wonder how many people in Baghdad phone to complain about the continuous noise of the daily funeral processions?

When you walk out on your deck and no longer smell the farm and country, it will be because the fields and forests have been replaced with concrete and asphalt. Will you move again?

So next time you smell that manure, take a deep breath, it will clear your sinuses for a week. At least that's what McGregor says.

Frustrated in Brookswood

My kids gave me a new barbecue as a retirement/birthday present. They didn't pay the extra $25.00 to have it assembled as they figured "the old man needs something to do."

Not a problem, I marinated some steaks, and figured in about 45 minutes I would hear the sizzle of sirloin on the gleaming, stainless steel Century 2000.

Four hours later, I ate my steaks. Now, I believe that the barbecue industry does not actually want people assembling their own "outdoor modular kitchen appliances". I could imagine the following conversation taking place between Dave, the new young apprentice and Bob, the wily veteran of instruction manual preparation. "Gee Bob, these instructions are somewhat confusing and yet it says they are easy to follow."

"Well Dave, you see, the retailers of our products don't make a lot of mark up so we don't want the buyer to put it together; we want them to support the economy and have the retail store do it. These are tough times and the best way to become a small business man in Canada is to buy a big business and wait six months." "I see Bob, but some of these steps are out of place and the pictures of the different sizes of nuts and bolts all look the same."

"That's right, Dave. You notice page three; that whole page is a schematic and burner placement chart, but it is for the natural gas model only. We don't mention that until right at the bottom of the page in small print so he'll have to start over. Frustration is what drives them back to the dealer."

"Now Bob, I noticed you took one of the ST4.2 self-tapping screws out of the package. The buyer won't be able to attach side panels EA and EB to back panel DB without all four."

"Think of the economy again. He will look for one all over his workbench and the drawer in the kitchen, and then go the local hardware store. He can only buy ST4.2 screws in a package of six and it is a proven fact that once in the hardware store he will buy something for his car, his tool box, and at least 1 item off the 50% off rack by the till. Then on the way home he'll swing by the beer store and we have generated some more revenue.

"Bob, the wire is too short leading to the self-igniter." "They are only a selling feature, if they were supposed to work we wouldn't drill a hole in the side to stick a match in."

"Bob have you always worked in the barbecue industry?" "No Dave I worked for years in the automotive industry, finding places under dashboards to hide turn signal flashers or designing light bulbs so people would eventually have to take the parts they bought to a dealership to have them installed. We have to keep people employed!"

"But Bob, how are people going to know it is better to get the thing assembled by the retailer?"

"We count on at least one frustrated person in each community writing a letter to the local paper to get the word out!"

Pay the extra $25.00. At least that's what McGregor says.

Spring Storms

Little Johnny was asked to spell the word "weather". He stood and recited, 'W-H-T-H-E-H-T-E-R." The teacher replied, "My, that's the worst spell of weather we've had in a long time!" We've also had a pretty bad spell of weather in the last few months, but most of us have forgotten about it already.

My friends in Burns Lake and Prince George tell me that when we get a few centimeters of snow down here they gather around the TV at 6 P.M. to watch the news. They particularly watch for two clips, the lady in the high heels with the umbrella talking on the cell phone picking her way through the slush and, the drivers on the Coquitlam hill that come over one by one and slide into the pile of cars at the bottom. It's better than Funniest Home Videos. They also point out to the 4X4 owners that, just because your tires say 'Off Road' doesn't mean your vehicle should be on its roof with your tires off the road!

We are Lower Mainlanders and we know winter will not last, so we don't prepare and we don't worry. The waters will recede, the winds will die down, the snow will melt, and the crocuses will bloom. As long as McDonalds and Starbucks don't lose power, we are fine, thank-you! A research company asked some people in southern B.C. to respond to a poll that showed we were apathetic. Most of them replied, "Who cares!?"

I live in an isolated part of the community called Brookswood. Sometimes, late at night, when it's quiet, my neighbours and I can hear snowplows off in the distance, but we've never really seen one. We don't complain, we shovel and scrape our driveways and slip and slide through the stop signs and we help each other out. Push a car here, jump-start a neighbour there, we get by. We know there is no Canadian FEMA, it will be our local Police, Fire, Public Works and ESS volunteers that come to help. So we make casseroles, fill the school gym with furniture and clothes, set up trust funds or organize telethons and we get it done while we wait for the sun to come out.

Right now, we've been teased with some nice spring weather again. Even though the stores have replenished their supplies of sidewalk salt, de-icer and anti-freeze, we walk right by the displays, we'll pick some up in September and be ready for next winter, (But we won't will we?). There is no need to buy snow tires now, after all its February in Langley, and we should be looking at prices on lawn mowers. Those trees that threatened our houses in the wind, well, they look pretty sturdy now. Maybe we'll get a price on topping them in the summer. (But we won't will we?)

I'm always impressed with the way our community comes together when faced with any adversity. We are helpers and fixers and doers and that is part of our make-up, real Canadians are not whiners.

But, there are two or three good storms to come before now and the end of March, get a price on the tires. At least, that's what McGregor says.

Spring Clean- Up

It was the first nice weekend of the year and the people on my street were attempting to break the Guinness World Record for 'most noise produced by a residential neighbourhood!'

Lawn mowers argued with chain saws, the buzz of weed eaters bounced off the fences in a cacophony of clatter with hedge trimmers. A rotor-tiller tried to drown out a leaf blower and at least two sizes of pressure washers sang out in shrill harmony. No one was sleeping in today.

Now someone will no doubt point out that manufacturers are now producing more environmentally safe electric, even cordless, quiet yard tools. I'm sorry, but men will not buy power tools if they don't make noise!

Take the pressure washer for instance. That is truly a man's tool. Noise, pressure, stripping, peeling, flushing, are all at the tip of your fingers. You put on your boots, gloves goggles, and you might as well be firing up a Harley and following Peter Fonda and Dennis Hopper into the desert. What is that grunt that Tim the Tool Man makes?

Surrounded by vibration and noise, you get lost in your own little world. You might be stripping grime from ten feet of sidewalk but it could be the deck of an aircraft carrier! She asks you to blast the moss off the planters, but in your mind you're flushing sludge off a 440 cu.in. muscle car engine, oh yeah! When you shut it off, the only sounds are water droplets slipping from the siding and rusty rivulets running down the driveway drain. It all looks so good!

Now, just suppose we had pressure washers for the body and mind. Put it on wide spray and peel a few inches and pounds off that gut. Next, a straighter stream to cut some definition in those abs and pecs, yes that looks great! Boy, this a lot cheaper than liposuction. Trim that big butt, peel those thunder thighs and carve those calves.

I'm sure such a device would have an attachment to go up into the aorta. Once inside there, put it on high pressure and start stripping out the cholesterol, plaque, and nicotine from the arteries and veins. Then, clear a path up into the heart. Swirl it around in all four chambers and rinse out the fat and crud. Now watch the blood race through there!

While we're in the mood, move up into the mind. Whoa! What a mess! When was the last time this was cleaned? Move all those old ideas out of the way. Spray away the cobwebs, the prejudice, and the negativity. Over in the corner we see piles of apathy and lumps of laziness to be blasted out. Up top is a huge clump of procrastination, hey leave it, we can get that tomorrow.

Look at all the room we've freed up for new ideas and clear thinking. Shut it off, stand back and take a look. Wow, we should have bought one of these machines years ago!

Yes, if we maintained our bodies and minds with the same pride and intensity we clean our yards and belongings, our personal resale value may increase at the same rate as our houses! Let's put some pressure on ourselves, and clean up, inside and out. At least, that's what McGregor says.

The Garaģe Sale

In the months of March and April, daffodils and tulips signal the welcome return of spring. The first warm weekend of May, the garage sale signs push up through the boulevards and sprout from the telephone poles, a sure sign that summer is nigh.

I don't often buy at garage sales but I enjoy wandering among the people and listening to the bartering and dealing as the suburban driveways are converted into Middle Eastern bazaars for the weekend.

"Does this work?" he asks, holding up a rare 20th century Radio Shack alarm clock. "It works fine!" replies the seller. What is he going to say, "No the alarm is screwed and the volume knob is broken." You'll find that out when you get it home. One rule of life, never buy any anything electric at a garage sale.

Now my studies have shown me that we have three basic types of events, The Yard Sale, the Garage Sale/ Moving Sale, and the Estate Sale. There are some distinct differences between the three.

The yard sale's purpose is to get rid of stuff they don't want. The garage sale is being held for a reason. Maybe they are renovating or moving and they need the room and want to make some money for the new bathroom tile or help pay the movers. The estate sell is more sophisticated, children reluctantly offering mom or dad's or Grandpa and Grandma's belongings to the public.

At the yard sale, a set of golf clubs and a mouldy bag will go for forty bucks. At the garage sale, clubs and bag with cart will be between $50.00 and $150.00 and at an estate sale Grandpa's polished Wilson irons and woods will be $450.00.

A Yard sale will have three dainty, flowered tea cups for 50 cents each.. At the garage sale there will be the same cups in a set of four with saucers for five dollars each and at the estate sale, there will be the full set with a matching tea pot that Grandma always served Sunday tea from and the entire set will go for $75.00-$100.00.

As the sellers discuss the day's sales they will invariably tell about "The Dealers" that came by at 8:30. They say "dealers' in a way that you can imagine men in trench coats with mirrored sunglasses getting out of black SUVs to rape and pillage the treasures lining the carport walls. Anything they steal will end up on Antiques Road Show for sure!

The small items, books, toys, CDs, move well as do tools and some small furniture. People squeeze by the exercise equipment trying not to let it touch them for fear it might rub off. Most of the exercise bikes still have the instruction manual hanging from the handlebars, just one more New Year's resolution gone bad.

On Sunday afternoon, the Yard sale is done around 2 PM, unsold items are marked FREE at the roadside and the proceeds have been converted to beer and pizza. The other sales hang on to the bitter end marking items down, wishing the dealers would come back.

Fill up your travel mug; check out the sales, I know that one thing you've been looking for is out there; at least that's what McGregor says!

Time to Get Rid of the Clutter

I caught the tail end of a talk show the other day, the guest was a "Clutter Expert" with tips on how to free up space in your home. The next day at the doctor's office, the Reader's Digest opened to an article titled *You Can Be a Clutter Cutter*. I took this as a sign from the universe and began to contemplate the state of emergency existing in my house.

A couple of years ago on a hot August afternoon, I was cleaning off my dining room table because my insurance man was coming over. The table doubles as a horizontal filing cabinet so I sorted the paid bills from the unpaid, the file folders and flyers from the unfinished poetry and piled them neatly on the bed in the spare room. My son came in as I was applying a coat of Pledge to the table, and asked, "Is it Thanksgiving today?" Well that about says it all, doesn't it?

The article says that most of our real clutter is the result of emotional clutter, attachments we can't break. This theory is put forth by a lady who is the President of the Professional Organizers of Canada! Can you imagine living with a lady with that title?

I can hear an interview with her husband, "Well, when we met I knew she was Mrs. Right, I just didn't know her first name was Always! When I go to the bathroom in the middle of the night she gets up and makes my side of the bed." I'm sure underwear left on the floor of that bedroom results in marriage counselling.

I had an organized neighbour; his garage was a shrine for all men. Bright fluorescent lighting accented white pegboard on every wall with outlines of each tool so he knew if one was missing. He borrowed my wheelbarrow once and when he brought it back he pointed out the rust spots he had sprayed with primer and noted that the wheel hadn't been greased in a long time! Now, guys, how many of you have ever chipped away the hardened concrete on your wheelbarrow looking for the grease nipple?

The article says to start small, so I chose a cupboard in my kitchen. There was an electric wok, a regular wok, a crock-pot, a waffle iron, a popcorn maker, a sandwich maker and a meat slicer I don't think is mine. The President says if I haven't used it in a year, get rid of it. I could take them to Penny Pincher, then, if I did need one of them I could go buy it, sort of like paying them to be a mini storage.

But, I am a Pisces, by nature a dreamer not a doer. I can write you a wonderful poem or story about clean up, but never get around to doing it, or if I start, I'm easily called away. But back to the clutter, all this stuff is now sitting on my kitchen floor, ready to be emotionally and physically discarded. But, I may use that sandwich maker now that I know where it is, so I'll put it back and I should keep one of the woks and I know someone will come looking for their meat slicer.

I'll just put them all back in. You shouldn't try to do too much the first time, at least that's what McGregor says.

Celebrating May Day

"Come lasses and lads, get leave of your dads, and away to the maypole hie; for every fair has a sweetheart there and the fiddler's standing by." This old English minstrel tune calls us all to the 86th annual May Day Festival in Fort Langley on Monday. But for me, that tune is also a reminder of my stint as a May Pole Dancer.

Fifty years or so ago, I was selected as one of the students to represent Langley Central Elementary in the Annual May Day May pole dance competition. Students from Coglhan, Wix-Brown, Murrayville, South Carvolth, Otter, Willoughby, Fort Langley and others all participated each year. Once again this year, there will be May pole dancing at the Fort as part of the long celebrated Victoria Day tradition.

Now regardless of what some of you may be thinking, May Pole dancing is not for sissies. On the school playground we had a practice pole with ribbons attached surrounded by a worn down ring of grass. I can assure you, that practice ring was no place for the weak. You see, back then this was big stuff. A record player and extension cord would be brought out and a very scratchy record placed on the turntable and we would be put through our paces by a well-experienced May Pole teacher. (I'm not certain, but there were rumours that off-season trades were made to bring in a teacher with May pole experience.)

You had to be more than just fleet of foot; there were many designs that had to be mastered. The braids in the weave design had to tight; the sections of the spider web design had to be symmetrical and the bows and the curtsies had to be on time and properly executed or marks were lost for sure. To un-weave the designs, you had to reverse or even skip backwards. I'm sure I was 'moon walking' long before Michael Jackson was even born.

There were hazards and distractions during training. Often the teacher/coach would get off beat with her clapping and dancers would be thrown off cadence, tangling ribbons and ankles at the same time. Rodney, the class clown, (who should never have been selected in the first place but his Mom was on the PTA) would purposely step on your heel until your shoe came off, and the bossy red haired girl was always shouting instructions telling us steps contrary to the teacher/coach.

But the day came and with the boys in grey slacks, white shirts and bow ties, and the girls in pretty dresses we performed well and no one fell down. I don't remember if we won but we all got a ticket for a cold Mission Orange pop and a hot dog. You can taste it can't you? Also I got to hold hands with Carol, a pretty girl in the next grade up, very cool.

This year, I'm sure the kids will have trained as hard and look just as sharp. There will be a parade with dainty baton twirlers and noisy antique tractors, come and watch and cheer. I know I always harp on getting involved but just showing up is easy to do, dancers need an audience, a parade needs people on the sidewalk, and you'll enjoy the day.

Put some fried onions on that hot dog, then it really tastes like a fair; at least that's what McGregor says.

Curling

I think we went through all four seasons at my house on the Easter weekend. But there was lots of variety on the 'things to do' list, both inside and outside, and when it was time to sit, there was golf, hockey, baseball and curling to watch.

I enjoy the March and April curling extravaganzas, the Canadian Championships followed by the World's. Canada is always in the running and I am a much better curler on my couch than I ever was at the rink.

I believe that everyone who professes to be a Canadian should have curled at least once to have a genuine piece of Canadian culture on their resume On every citizenship test there should be at least one curling related question such as: In the sport of Curling the term 'Hack' refers to A. indentions in the ice used as foot holds when shooting the rocks B-A loud annoying coughing sound you make just as your opponent is releasing their rock C-A large star shaped crack made in the ice by your rock when you stumble on delivery.

If you have not curled before it is a combination of shuffleboard, billiards and bowling and then some clown decided it should be played on ice. You shoot from one set of rings, called the house, to another house at the other end. I think it is called the house because once you get hooked on the game you spend more time there than at home. After four members of each team throw two rocks each, the closest to the center circle scores. That is a quick explanation, there are lots of other rules developed by warring clans in Scotland that for some reason still exist today.

A team consists of four persons. The lead is usually a quiet person who is a smarter and better curler than the skip but just likes to be part of the team and knows his rocks don't usually contribute to the outcome. He probably was a skip but got tired of all the blame being heaped on his shoulders. The second is a smarter and better curler than the skip but likes his position because he can often rocket a take-out down the ice without it costing them any final points. The third is also smarter and a better curler than the skip, but has the advantage of saying, seven or eight times a game, 'Well, you're the skip, it's your decision.'

The skip knows the only two rocks that are important are his, but needs the others so he doesn't have to throw all eight. Besides, the other three are usually relatives, coworkers or neighbours so he has to tolerate them. I curled with my Dad, my uncle and my brother one year. We curled for two hours on Monday and didn't talk to each other for the next four days.

Do not confuse the slick, well-oiled robotic like curling teams on TV with recreational curlers. On TV, when the skip yells 'Sweep!', the sweepers are poised and ready for action, gliding beside the rock. In the recreational leagues when the skip shouts that command, it is not unusual that his sweepers are watching an exciting shot on the next sheet, sharing pictures of grandkids or just plain tuckered out.

It is a fun sport to learn; be a Canadian, take your family curling. At least that's what McGregor says.

Stumps and Seeds

Finally some May weather is here and we can get outside and start on those outdoor projects. Dad always used the 24th of May as his planting benchmark, an old prairies adage. The last week of May was usually warm enough and dry enough to plant and yet still allowed an adequate growing season.

In B.C., outdoor projects historically start in the second week of May, which always coincides with the Canucks removal from the Stanley Cup Playoffs. After all, there is no longer any reason to sit inside on a nice evening and swear at your TV so you might as well be outside enjoying the fresh spring air.

The neighbour and I took out a scraggly mature cedar hedge and plan to replace it with a fence. It was actually no longer a hedge, just a row of neglected, gnarly old cedar trees. I gave the boys the task of digging out the stumps and roots. They dug and chopped and developed a system that had them out in a week and they did a good job. It only cost me an axe, a shovel handle and about $80.00 worth of pizza, McDonalds and Coke.

There was one large stump that I told them to leave; I would get it out. I don't do a lot of digging or chopping any more these days so I wrapped a chain around it, hooked the other end to my truck and hauled it out. After all, if a guy has a stump, a chain and a pick-up truck, it is only a matter of time until the three of them come together in some combination.

After the stump comes out you can stand over it with your work gloves and boots on and savour a pioneer moment. You recall those old black and white images of sweat stained farmers yelling at a team of horses or oxen as they strain on a huge stump that has to go. Or even more macho are pictures of dirt and debris flying from the stumping powder explosions. Alas, using a stick of dynamite in a residential neighbourhood is frowned upon today.

Working outdoors is great therapy. It's great time to think, to wrestle with a challenge or a decision that's been rolling around in your mind. As you are cutting and pruning branches you can chop off some tired old ideas, shape your thoughts so they grow in a new direction. As the tiller or the hoe turn over the weeds and pull up fresh new earth, you can yank out those ugly old habits and fears that have been holding you back.

Mowers and weed-eaters and tillers don't talk back or give advice. They just listen as you lay out thoughts and rearrange them until you reach a decision. I worked for an organization once that had a thick, comprehensive policy manual. On the very last page they had written in bold, 'If a situation arises that is not covered in this manual, do the right thing.'

Usually you already know how your situation should come out, but outside, shedding the winter, picking up the debris from the storms, planting new seeds and encouraging growth, you can see the new path and head in the new direction.

But if those old ideas just don't want to leave, wrap a chain around them and pull them out by the roots. At least that's what McGregor says.

Pot Holes and Detours

I came across a quote the other day: 'The road to success is always under construction.' Well if that's true Langley is going to be very successful because it seems like almost every road I travel these days is being torn apart, raised, lowered, widened or bridged.

Of course, spring and summer months are always when any major changes are made to our infrastructure. It only makes sense to do major repairs when the climate is going to permit digging and trenching and paving.

But this year, even the detours seem to direct us from one construction project to another until it seems we are going around in circles. The signs are not much help. When you see a flashing board that says, 'Traffic Pattern Change Ahead,' all you can be really sure of is that it is going to take you ten minutes longer to get where you are going.

You have to rely on the flag persons and you have to pay attention. If they smile at you as you drive by, you have adapted to the new traffic pattern and made them happy. However, if they are shaking their heads, scowling, and pointing at their signs, you have done something stupid. Usually, you have been looking elsewhere other than the paddle she is holding. These ladies know that, unfortunately, men turn into little boys when there are big trucks and machines working and they tend to be glancing at the construction and heading into the oncoming traffic.

I have done my share of traffic control and I can assure you that flashing lights on fire trucks, ambulances and police cars are even more of a draw than backhoes or bulldozers. It is a scary feeling when you are standing in the traffic wearing reflective clothing, holding a flashlight and waving a reflective traffic paddle and the car is coming straight for you because the driver is looking at the accident. When they finally do look at you they are usually annoyed that they had to slow down.

Detours throw off the entire day. For example, we once had 200th St. blocked off at 56th Ave. because a motor home was burning in the two southbound lanes. I stopped a young lady as she tried to drive past and she said, "But I have to go to Brookswood." I told her the road would be closed for some time. Again, she advised me that 'that is how I get to Brookswood.' I told her she would have to go east but I didn't mention she should turn south at 203rd. I imagine she was well past Hope two hours later.

Please just leave our routes alone. We want to go the same way every day and we don't want our tidy streets turned to freeways. But when it is all done, it looks great, we move faster and we forget about the temporary inconvenience. If the Township Engineering Department had called it the '208th St. Corridor Enhancement,' no one would have shown up at the public meeting. But nobody wants a Truck Route. If you name something a Greenway, a Beltway or a Parkway it sure sounds a lot quieter than a freeway.

Take the road less travelled; enjoy the detour. The next time you're stopped inconveniently at a construction site remember, we don't have to worry about mortars or IEDs in our roadways. At least that's what McGregor says.

Just a Teaser

Last weekend was a 'teaser weekend.' Every year we get a couple of these in March and April and we always seem to get caught in their deception. Weekends like these are full of lies and misdirection making promises that they have no intention of fulfilling.

We watched puffy white clouds drift lazily overhead headed for the interior. They casually gave us the impression that they have finished dumping snow or sleet or continuous rain and that they are just passing by. If you listened close you could hear a disrespectful snicker as they floated up the valley. March clouds are not to be trusted.

The wind was nothing more than a gentle rustle. There was no danger of branches falling or power outages. The only sound was a quiet whisper encouraging us to start cleaning up the yard, picking up branches and deadfall, raking the lawns or dragging out the pressure washer. The wind looked us straight in the eye and said "I'm done for the winter, go ahead and haul all that stuff away, sprinkle on some fertilizer and grass seed, you can get a good early start on the growing season this year." Lies, all lies.

The sun reached down and massaged our neck and shoulders, relieving the knots and cramps caused by being hunched in hoodies and rain jackets for the last few months. "Doesn't that feel good?" old Sol asks in a soft warm voice. "You can go ahead and put those heavy coats, socks and gloves away, you won't need them anymore this year. Soon it will be daylight saving time and I will be so much more pleasant. By the way, why don't you take those noisy snow tires off, you won't need them again this year. Go ahead, organize some baseball practices and soccer tournaments; it's time to get outside."

What a cruel mistress, that sun can be, casually yawning and stretching, promising to visit more often when it really has no intention of coming back for days or weeks. But just like Charlie Brown running to kick that football, we believe that this year will be different and we won't be fooled again.

So we roll up our sleeves and clean and wax and wash our houses, scour our decks and cars and trucks. We fold up sweaters and blankets, we take off our winter tires and we start digging around in flowerbeds, fully believing that the forces of nature have been honest with us. They watch, punching each other in the shoulder, laughing hysterically knowing that we have fallen for it once again.

Unsuspectingly, we will awaken one mid-March Wednesday morning to a dump of wet sloppy snow hanging from the branches and covering the roads. We will hear cars slipping and spinning and we'll search for the kid's boots and mittens.

The wind will blow in later in the day, melting the snow, snapping branches and make a complete mess of your yard again. The sun will be nowhere to be seen and the clouds will sit like huge bullies over top of us and refuse to move, rendering daylight saving time useless.

I have lived in the Fraser Valley for many years and I have learned to make the best of the spring days we are given. If the sun shines on a March day, get out and enjoy it, but don't believe a word it says. At least that's what McGregor says,

Setting Priorities

I did an assessment tour of my yard on a sunny weekend afternoon recently. This exercise is in no means making any commitment to actually do anything, but it is important to size up the tasks and prioritize and schedule the chores to eliminate any waste of time or energy.

Too many times we rush into jobs without any pre-planning and find ourselves saying, 'Darn, I should have measured that thing before I ordered those things." Taking the extra time at the assessment stage of a project can pay off in the end.

I could start cleaning and preparing all my flower beds but I've been thinking about getting some new topsoil so I might just as well wait until I get that so I'm not raking and digging twice. I'll have to check around for soil prices.

My sundeck needs a lot of work. The shade and rainwater have rotted some of the posts and the entire railing has to come off. The stairs are also wobbly. I have to decide what kind of decking I'm going to use and how that will impact the stair replacement. Maybe I should have someone a few grades up the carpenter scale to look at that project.

The new fence we put up last year should be painted or stained. The house also needs to be painted so should I buy a natural stain for the fence or get paint for the fence to match the trim on the house? I think I have some of those paint selection charts somewhere; I'll find them and take a look. It's too early in the year to paint anyhow.

I also think I need new windows. I'm the only one in the neighbourhood that doesn't have them and a friend suggested that the heat loss from my house alone could be accounting for our recent mild winters. I suppose I should put windows in before I paint. Look at the condition of those gutters too and the moss on the shady side of the roof isn't good. I'll have to get some prices.

That old freezer that found its way here has to go and so does that old truck rear end. Add to that a large pile of brush from last fall's pruning and I have a good load to go for salvage and the dump. I could load that up and swing by and get some topsoil on the way back. Good plan but it's too late in the day to start that.

My Dad's old wind chimes tinkle as a wisp of wind passes through. They hang from a fir tree by the picnic table just as they did at his place. Many sunny afternoons after a day of clean up we would sit there with coffee and pie after all the work was done. That memory reminds me there is another option here today. I don't have to do anything.

I make a cup of coffee and carry my Stephen King book out to the picnic table. The chimes chatter a welcome and I spend the rest of afternoon sitting in the sun reading.

Decision-making can be stressful. Setting priorities, establishing timelines and manpower requirements, choosing colors and styles can pile up heavily on top of us.

When this happens, it's not fun anymore. Sometimes the best option of all is just to do nothing. At least that's what McGregor says.

Playground Lessons

I stumbled on an article that made me shake my head, but not too hard, I didn't want to risk personal damage. It seems that on a school ground in Toronto, an adult was supervising noon hour activities and was smacked in the head by an errant soccer ball and suffered a concussion.

The administration of the school quickly called a meeting and they decided, to avoid any possibility of litigation they would act by banning the use of all inflatable balls on the school ground. Boy, I can just imagine the group surrounding that table.

No doubt the majority had suffered some traumatic playground experiences in their youth, getting pounded in dodge ball, getting stuffed in lockers, or being beaned at the plate during a game of noon hour baseball. Now was their chance to get those dreaded balls off the playground.

In other cases, games of tag have been banned so as not to "bruise anyone's self-esteem" and in even more drastic cases, playgrounds have been removed altogether so that no one gets hurt. Of course the Child Psychologists had to become involved.

One professional expert noted that risk taking is important in the development of children and that children learn to overcome fear gradually by being able to measure their own abilities and learn new ones by successes and failures.

For instance, if you throw a punch and end up on your butt with a black eye, you learn to write poetry instead of buying boxing gloves. If you can't climb the rope in the gym all the way to the top, you pursue a more academic curriculum, and if you keep getting smacked in the head with an inflatable ball on the playground, you spend more time at administrative meetings instead of supervising outside. The playground is very educational.

The point is, children have to be allowed to test their skills, face their fears and eventually learn how high they can climb, how fast they can run and far they can jump. The same experts tell us that children who are hurt in scrapes and falls before the age of nine, are less likely to be afraid to fall or get hurt as teenagers. Who would have thought that saving our kids from harm could be harmful?

The fear of someone getting hurt drives the paranoia of lawsuits and too often people overreact, fearful that it will cost them. Boy, was I an idiot. Many years ago I was coaching Little League and called for the boys to throw in the ball not knowing two boys had baseballs. One hit squarely in my glove the other broke my nose and knocked me out for a minute or two.

After a crunching nasal rearrangement and some stitches, I apologized to the boy and his family. I was an adult coach in charge of these kids and I should have been paying attention. I could have sued them and made a bundle, but in the old days, games were games and we learned as much from our losses as we did from our wins.

Yes, I did end up writing poetry with an administrative job. You shouldn't have to be hit in the head too many times to learn where you belong.

To all you administrators and lawyers out there, spend more time on your budgets and your felons and let the kids be kids. At least, that's what McGregor says.

Jim McGregor

The Joy of Gardening

I had great intentions of working in the yard, just doing some pruning and edging, a bit of clean up. However, I found myself standing at the kitchen window watching the hail wage 'shock and awe' onto the buds and blossoms, so I watched movie instead.

This is a frustrating time of year for people with green thumbs, they are twitching and itching to get back outside and get growing. Even if it's applying some lime or raking out moss, they will find yard work to do. A good option to actually doing the work is going to the garden center to think about doing the work.

I rummaged through a kitchen drawer and found a gift card from one of our great local garden spots and decided to get a quick gardening fix. Just walking through you can smell the plants, hear the display waterfalls and catch some warmth seeping through the greenhouse. It all looks so healthy and colourful, and it will look so great in your yard.

You can spot the difference between the true gardeners and the weekend weeders. The gardeners are the ones buying the right stuff to put on the right stuff, they watch The Garden Show every Saturday morning and they know both the common names and the Latin names for all the plants in their yards. You will never hear them ask for 'something red to go beside my white things.' They know when to sew and when to reap.

But you don't even need to hear them talk to recognize a gardener. They come to the garden center in their garden clothes. The faded pants, baggy shirts, slip on boots or shoes and a hat that is stained from sweat on the inside and rain on the brim. They are prepared to lift bags or pots or shovel dirt. They pass by the pretty petal packaged garden tools and wrap their hands around the ergonomic handles of hoes or weeders. They are in training for the upcoming season. It won't be long now, soon the temperature will climb, the gun will sound and we're off.

Now critics will tell me that I can buy vegetables cheaper than growing them, but the gardening experience is much better than driving, parking and bustling shoulder to shoulder in a noisy market. It is positively therapeutic to stand in a vegetable garden early in the morning, hose in one hand and coffee in the other.

A believe a garden reflects a lot about a person's character. Some gardeners will have perfectly straight rows, well-manicured edges, no weeds, perfect bean poles. My garden is not like that. It is somewhat orderly and yet a bit scattered, as I said it reflects the gardener. The pumpkins are for the grandkids and nieces and nephews, the parsnips stay in the ground 'til Christmas day, the peas are planted by my son and disappear shortly after filling on the vines, and the rest is for me or given away.

I buy a Farmer's Almanac every year and in that book of wisdom I gain many gardening tips, like handling pests such as rabbits or slugs. Slugs are pests and I am convinced that they can move with lightning speed after dark, devouring complete rows in one night. One tip from the book is to put out a saucer of beer to attract them. I don't think this kills them but they are drunk and hung over in the morning and, like your old roommate, easier to remove.

My only concern is that, sure, it starts with one innocent saucer of beer for your slugs and then slugs from other yards show up uninvited and you have a 'slugfest!' It's all fun until a potato loses and eye!

Speaking of potatoes, I always have "volunteers" growing in among my carrots. Obviously left behind from last year and tumbled around by the tiller in the spring. They usually do better than the seed potatoes I bought. No problem, I figure the potatoes and carrots are going to end up on the plate side by side so why not grow in the same row together.

Maintenance is a tedious chore, and often I have left it too long and don't take time to differentiate plants from weeds. I have a tip for you. If you aren't sure if something is a weed or a valuable plant, pull on it. If it comes out easily, it was valuable plant. Hence the reason some of my rows look like the smile of an NHL hockey star, a few gaps here and there.

The Almanac tells me, "A few rays of sunshine for pleasure, a sprinkle of raindrops for mirth, a man is closer to God in a garden, than anywhere else on Earth!"

Plant the seeds. Nature pretty much looks after the rest. At least, that's what McGregor says.

Jim McGregor

Country Harvest

Scenes from a Farmer's Market

Pick-ups piled, packed with produce,
Pumpkins, pears and peach for pies;
People poke and pick their purchase,
Proudly paying penny-wise.

Picasso painted pansy palettes
Producing powerful perfumes;
Peonies with pretty petals
Pretending to be peacock plumes.

Potatoes, parsnips, pickles, peppers,
Planters, pastries, parsley, peas;
Preserves from plaza to the pantry
Painstakingly prepared to please.

Pedestrians pause and pester peddlers,
Plucking plump and purple plums,
Placed by pots of pink petunias,
Pushing past protruding 'mums.

Parcels, packages placed in packsacks,
Pick-ups plundered, pull away;
A potpourri of precious pictures,
Promise all a pleasant, perfect day!

Bike Professionals

I was out for a walk on perfect evening. My massage therapist says I need exercise for my sore back. I was hoping to hear her tell me to lie on a heating pad for a month but apparently I have to build up my core. I patted my stomach showing her that my core was indeed getting bigger but she was not amused.

She says the years have caught with me after changing truck and tractor tires and responding to adrenaline-fuelled emergencies. Personally, I believe the pain is the result of bending over backwards to please everyone all my life, but no one else supports that theory.

The neighbourhood was quiet, particularly no kids. No hockey nets, no bikes or skateboards, no arguments or noise. The dynamics of a neighbourhood change as kids grow and leave. I can recall my kids running in yelling for a loony because the ice cream truck was coming. Today, an ice cream truck drove down the street and no one came out.

I walked past the school playground and the still swings were casting long shadows across the slides and monkey

49

bars. The soccer field and baseball diamonds were empty. What a waste of a beautiful evening.

Later that night my Buddy Brian sent me an article from the Calgary Herald written by Naomi Lakritz. Everyone once in a while Brian does this to bait me, and it usually inspires a column. The article tells us that parents can now hire 'professionals' to come and teach their kids to ride bikes without training wheels. This company is called Pedalheads and their theory is that parents are too busy and 'getting a pro gives kids a supportive environment and is safer and more fun.'

Riding a bike used to be something you had to do if you wanted to keep up with everyone. Your parents, brothers or sisters or a friend held the seat and let you go and off you went. It wasn't about safety or being supportive it was about survival and getting those bloody training wheels off was a big deal.

I remember when they paved Norris Road. No more gravel or potholes and every kid on that street from the McGregors at one end down to the Muenchs at the other end rode back and forth on that smooth black pavement for hours until it was dark.

When it was dark I can recall flying down that fresh blacktop and the only sound was the generator purring on my back tire making that handlebar light brighter than ever. What a feeling of freedom on a cool night after a hot summer day as the wind went rushing by and I was sure I was going to break the sound barrier. I did all of this without professional training.

This professional service has been available in the Lower mainland for years apparently and I wonder if they also teach lessons in hopscotch or marbles. Maybe they have a Power Point Presentation on how to play hide and seek or tag as well.

Maybe the kids have been so busy at their organized sports activities they are tired at the end of the day. I hope they get a chance to experience playing outside after dark. Maybe parents should hire a professional to come in and yell at the kids: "Turn that bloody TV off and go play outside!" At least that's what McGregor says.

Jim McGregor

Blowing in the Wind

The City of Oak Bay is reportedly looking at banning the use of leaf blowers in residential areas of the City. The people supporting this decision cite problems with being exposed to extreme sustained levels of high-pitched noise and an excess of exhaust emissions. I think a lot of cranky old seniors must live in Oak Bay.

Wouldn't you know that I just recently bought my first leaf blower and now people are starting movements to ban them? I bought one for a couple of reasons. Firstly, I have a lot of leaves and needles that collect in drains and gutters and secondly, most of my neighbours have one.

It is very embarrassing to be outside on a Saturday morning with a push broom and a dustpan when others are blowing gravel or sucking up debris from their lawns with no effort at all. Sure, they would politely wave and smile at my 19th century method of dust removal but I knew what they are thinking.

When I finally made the decision to buy one, I did some investigation into price, rpm, weight, and size. There was quite a selection to choose from and a guy has to spend a lot of time examining the features. After all, it's a lot like a new car. Once it appears in your driveway, your neighbours will give it the once over and either shake their heads or give it a thumbs up.

One of the big decisions is to whether to go with gas or electric. They both make noise but if I am concerned about the environment I'm leaving my grandchildren, the electric may be the better choice given that gasoline is fast approaching a buck fifty per litre.

My in depth blower analysis reveals that I can purchase an electric blower with an equivalent rpm to the gas model with more features, including the vacuum conversion, at less cost. I already have a long extension cord and I will be saving money not having to buy gas.

With my new toy safely in my garage, my next consideration is when and where to use it. Knowing that I am having some tree work done, I figure I should wait until that has been completed. One of the concerns in the proposed Oak Bay noise bylaw is the restriction on times when blowers can and cannot be used.

Certainly, I don't want to be out there too early and no one wants to hear one buzzing away in the quiet evening hours. Shortly after 8:30 on any given Saturday in my neighbourhood, the chain saws, mowers, pressure washers and leaf blowers all start at once as if a conductor in a grand orchestra has waved his baton.

I decide just after lunch I will take my seat in the blower section of this ensemble and after a bit of very simple assembly I am plugged in and ready to blow.

Thirty seconds in my blower stops. I look around and see the cord has caught on one of Noma garden lights. I straighten the light and plug it back in. Thirty seconds later, the cord has caught on my brick planter and it stops again. I look around and don't see anyone watching but I know they're out there.

Depression sets in as I realize, to heck with the environment, I should have bought the gas one. At least that's what McGregor says.

I Can do That Tomorrow

I was happy to have a dreary, rainy weekend. As a world-class procrastinator I have been putting a lot of things off. I was behind in some projects I had taken on for other people and the deadlines were getting closer. Even though, like a lot of people, I do my best work under pressure, I had been finding lots of ways to put things on the back burner.

The rain was partially my fault. I had spent an hour Friday afternoon washing and vacuuming my truck and I had it looking good so of course now I'd had to drive through puddles whenever I went out.

But the rain meant I wouldn't be able to pick up the windfall of branches or power rake the moss or cut the grass or pressure wash everything that doesn't move. My neighbours have been doing that sort of stuff and I personally think they have started too early in the year because now their yards look better than mine and it makes for a long season of trimming and primping.

So after a healthy breakfast, I put on some easy listening music, adjusted my chair and fired up my computer. I was ready to work and clean up that file on the edge of the desk.

I prepare a quarterly newsletter for an organization I belong to so I opened my Publisher program, which I have just mastered and now find out it is out of date. "There are better programs," I am told but if they involve learning new procedures and processes, they are not easier to me.

I type in "Winter 2015" at the top of page one, then feeling a tad guilty. I change that to "Spring 2015". Maybe there won't be quarterly newsletter this year. I'll go for quality rather than quantity, so I change "Spring" to "April" because it will be April by the time they get it anyway.

I am ready to paste in the first article I had received and I click on the file to retrieve it. Now, what name did I save that under? After 15 frustrating minutes I find it under the sender's name instead off the document title. Of course the next document I look for is saved under the title not the sender's name.

I have some pictures on a USB drive to go with one of the articles and I know the drive was on my desk but everything from the living room was plunked on that desk during the carpet episode so I'm going to have to move some of that stuff first. But I need a coffee.

Now you can see why most of high school papers came back, "C-, Jim would have received a higher mark if he had handed his work in on time."

Experts say the best way to beat procrastination is to break a big project down into smaller, more manageable segments, like "Saturday, finish page 1, Monday finish page 2 etc." and this makes sense to me. After all page 1 is done now, is it not?

I push the all - important 'save' button and close the document. I think curling is on in a few minutes.

It's supposed to rain the next day as well and I should be able to finish it. But if I eventually have to change it to Summer 2015, that's okay, too. At least that's what McGregor says.

What Are You Letting Grow?

I had some uninvited guests visit my back yard last summer. Some small patches of green ivy popped up in the ground cover under the trees. At first I thought they were fitting in well with the other residents, filling in some bare spots and cuddling up to the ferns and hostas. So I just let them stay.

It was mostly green back there and I had once thought about infusing some color between the yucca plants but then I decided, with fronds like that, who needs anemones? Nature always seemed to know just what my little jungle needed.

By fall, when everything else was dying off or going dormant for the winter, I noticed my guests were still growing strong and they had even started to work their way up the fir trees. It actually looked pretty, giving my forest an English garden look, and soon my back yard looked more like Oxford or Cambridge than Brookswood.

But it showed no signs of stopping and by spring it was crowding, choking and covering everything and it was now well up into the trees. After some investigation, I found that when this visitor had first appeared I should have said,

"Sorry, you're not welcome here. Move along." It seems this particular strain will develop a root system that robs nutrients from the tree roots, it attaches to the tree in such a way that it kills the bark and if it gets to the canopy, it blocks the photosynthetic process and the weight of the vine can bring the dead tree down.

I followed guidelines and donned a dusk mask, goggles and long sleeves and began the task of peeling it off and, on a couple of trees, it came off intact, a huge 50 foot ecosystem. I could almost hear the trees take a deep breath as the foliage fell to the ground. It was a lot of work but if I hadn't let it go so long, it wouldn't have been such a big task.

But that's human nature isn't it. We tend to leave things alone until the situation becomes critical. We let depression start around our feet and ignore it until it has covered our entire body, blocking out the sunshine.

We wait until the vines are squeezing our chests until we decide to do something to free up our hearts and lungs. We wait until our abuses or addictions have choked out and smothered the healthy life around us and then suddenly, we find ourselves starving for light.

The secret I found to rid these vines was to do some digging, find the root of the problem. Once I had the root firmly in my grasp, if I was careful I could pull it all away in one piece. In some cases it wasn't that easy. The invader had to be removed bit by bit, in small pieces. But the secret was to not give in to it.

Getting to the root of the problem is where you have to start. It may take getting down on your knees, it may take asking for help, it may mean getting dirty and you might not like what you find down there, but it's a good place to begin.

Summer is a good time to clean up your garden, your body and your mind. Take a close look at what you're letting grow in there. At Least that's what McGregor says.

Fruit Trees and Nature

I was browsing through the Township Events calendar recently and came across a course titled,' How to Train Your Fruit Trees to Produce More Fruit.' I was intrigued by this as I wasn't sure if you actually brought your fruit trees to the class and had them pay attention or if this was a course for the orchard owner.

It seems the workshop will cover how fruit trees grow and how to direct new growth to produce bigger crops in future years. Discussion will include training of various tree forms, fruit thinning of apples and pears, and the use of mesh bags as non-chemical barriers to prevent Codling Moth and Apple Maggot infestations of the fruit.

I have a pear tree and a cherry tree and I do absolutely nothing to them each and yet I always get pears and cherries. I don't do dormant spraying or add any fertilizers and the only pruning I do is loping off a low hanging branch if it interferes with the lawn mowing. Nature seems to look after all the other stuff.

No doubt there are many things I could do to increase the crop but I don't can or preserve anything and a juicy pear for dessert or a bowl of cherries as a snack is plenty for me and my two trees seem to appreciate the lack of attention.

I seem to recall that fruit grows on the previous year's growth so if you don't prune regularly, the fruit ends up on top where you can't reach it. Guys have ladders and being able to pick cherries standing on the ground sounds pretty boring to me. I like to think that nature knows what she's doing.

I recall a story about a man who stopped by his friend's house for a visit. He was distraught and depressed and embarrassed by the way his life had turned out. His friend was an avid gardener and suggested they go out to the rose garden where it was quiet.

Before he sat down the gardener plucked a rose bud, ready to open, from a bush and asked his troubled friend to open while he talked. His friend commiserated on the way his poor life had unfolded, trying to assign blame for his misfortune.

When he stopped talking, the gardener asked him how he was making out with the rose. It was a mess. The stem was broken the leaves were torn and most of the fragile petals were on the ground. "I messed it up," was the reply.

The gardener said, "Look around at the roses God has opened, how perfect they are, glowing and fragrant. Maybe you should stop trying to run your life the way you have been, give it to God and let him unfold it for you."

For centuries we have been grafting, cloning, spraying, pruning and clear-cutting everything nature has provided to us and yet here we are in the twenty-first century and we are told our planet is a mess. We choke the leaves with smog and chemicals and we poison the soils and waste the water and yet the trees still give us fruit in spite of how bad we have treated them.

I think the workshop that should be mandatory for all mankind is the one that teaches us, "How to Leave Things Alone and Let Nature Take its Course." At least that's what McGregor says.

Spring Clean up Can Be a Chore

Anyone with a piece of turf on this planet enjoys hearing there will be a week of nice weather in early spring. Getting a head start on yard and house clean-up is a bonus.

I set aside a day for pressure washing the deck, patio, stairs and railings and got outside early. The wind chimes were tinkling, the tulips were up, the cherry blossoms were out and the sun was already welcoming me from the clear blue sky.

I moved stuff around, sprayed on some cleaner and fired up the pressure washer and began blasting away the winter moss and mould. After about thirty minutes the fuel ran out and I stopped for a coffee and muffin, happy with the progress I had made. I refilled the tank, started the machine and it ran until I got to the top of the stairs and then quit.

I pulled the cord a few times but nothing happened; I played with the choke and pulled some more. I checked the plug and pulled, I checked the air filter and pulled. I was reminded of the story about the minister who was buying a lawn mower at a garage sale but it wouldn't start. The young man selling it said, "You have to swear at it." He replied, "I am a man of the cloth, I don't know any swear words." The boy replied, "You just keep pulling on that rope and they will come to you!"

I confess I did begin to curse, normally at first, then stringing words creatively together even fashioning some new combinations with each yank of that cord. Then I felt a sting and looked at my hand to see a blister had formed and popped. Adding to my frustration, those once calloused hands that changed truck tires or tossed hay bales all summer were now soft and tender as a baby's bum.

Now there was blood and sweat and tears could not be far away. Surely the devil had created the Briggs and Stratton engine.

I went in to clean it up and put a Band-Aid on and decided to check Google only to find I had done all the suggestions. The only thing left was to drain the gas and blow out the lines. That only proceeded to make more of a mess and dissolve the Band-Aid.

With the new gas in, I started pulling again but my finger hurt and now I have no idea how left handed people start air-cooled engines as it was not easy to pull the cord with my other hand. I got a glass of water and plunked down on the steps. My chest was pounding and I wondered how such a perfect day had suddenly turned out so bad.

Then I heard the wind chimes, I saw the tulips and the blossoms and felt the warm sun on my neck. The day hadn't changed at all, only I had. How frail we are that a honk of horn, an unkind word or a stubborn machine can affect our attitude in an instant. We are experts at bringing in our own dark clouds to cover the sun.

I took Satan's pressure washer to the repair shop, made some iced tea and sat on the clean half of my deck, feeling my heart rate return to normal. The rest can wait. Anger is just one letter short of 'danger.' At least that's what McGregor says.

Spring Baseball

The young mother tried to shield her face from the bitter wind but it seemed to be coming from all directions, biting and nipping at any exposed skin. At times the stinging rain would slice in sideways and find its way down her collar. She tried not to let her thoughts stray to the gloves, warm socks, scarves and boots she had left behind. She should have known better, but now she concentrated on keeping her fingers from going numb, marking strikes and balls on the scorebook. Spring baseball could be as close to hypothermia as you would ever want to be.

We all have memories of warm summer days, playing baseball in sun drenched parks while the spectators relaxed in the stands with cold drinks and ice cream. But realistically, the true baseball parent is one that survives early April and May games.

You never know what you are going to get as you leave for the park. If those dark clouds move east, you might have a decent, warm afternoon. If they stall overhead, be prepared for hail, sleet, thunder or any other type of winter weather system, but usually not bad enough for the coaches to cancel the game. If the sun does come out it is hot and you get burned on one side of your face if the bleachers aren't set right.

Moms will tough it out under blankets or umbrellas, cheering the team on and constantly looking at their watches. Dads don't normally suffer as bad. If the weather turns nasty, they retreat to the car, turn on the heater and Stanley Cup playoff game honking only occasionally to let the family know they saw the great catch and haven't succumbed to carbon monoxide poisoning.

There is a good reason for this. Mothers can bundle together in the stands and conserve and share their body heat; this is quite acceptable. However it can clearly damage a young boy's psyche forever if he were to look in from the outfield to see a bunch of fathers all snuggled together. This is just not acceptable on an athletic field, and it's better if Dad goes to the car.

This inclement weather is bad for the coach to. When he phones to say there is going to a practice or a re-scheduled game he always hopes the father will answer. The coach will say, 'Practice tomorrow five o'clock at City Park," and the father will say, "Five o'clock City Park, he'll be there." If Mom answers she will likely say, "It's supposed to rain." The coach will explain they have to get these practices or games in and Mom will say. "You don't do the laundry at your house do you? Do you expect those pants to stay white if you keep dragging them out into the mud?" The coach will never win this argument.

April and May include Easter long weekend and Mother's Day. It is not popular to schedule anything for those weekends. Even the year we had the boys give all their mothers a flower before the Mother's day game only gave us a small reprieve.

The prepared baseball mom packs an emergency kit in the trunk. It contains three layers of winter clothing, shorts, sandals and sunscreen so they can adapt as the day goes by.

The important thing to remember Mom, the kid's will remember you were there. At least that's what McGregor says.

Back Yard Burning

I was headed out to the Aldergrove recycling site with a truckload of braches and leaves, the last load of debris from my spring clean-up. As I drove along 16thAve., I was envious of those folks with large tracts of land that were still able to obtain burning permits. Every few miles there was another pile, flames crackling and spiralling up into the smoke. With the window down, I could get the odd whiff of cedar and fir being consumed.

There is something about feeding a fire, something awakens from deep in our past lives and the warmth comes from both the flames and the feeling of renewal, cleaning up, getting rid of the garbage.

Back yard burning used to be quite prevalent until the Regional District and a bunch of know it all, busy body Fire Chiefs (ironically, I was one of them!) stopped the practice because of environmental concerns. In reality, as the small houses with big lots disappeared and became apartment blocks or dead end roads became subdivision cul-de-sacs, the number of burning complaints increased. Not everyone needs that inner warmth.

The burning complaints were always a pain in the neck for whoever was the weekend Duty Officer. It was usually a neighbour, who didn't want to be identified, who would phone in the complaint. The homeowners never had permits but had lots of reasons for burning.

One gentleman told me one night that he had an ornamental tree that had a Japanese beetle fungus and the nursery had told him to burn the branches, not dispose of them. I asked him if the fence posts, paneling, two by fours and siding he was also burning had the Japanese fungus as well. They didn't so he was asked to let the fire die down.

A contractor one weekend had told the young labourer to start a fire and clean up the crap lying around. Now I'm sure he meant the wood scraps and the paper etc. but the eager young boy piled on vinyl siding, plastic, insulation and made a pile eight feet high.

When I arrived the fire was too big for the neighbours to get close to with garden hoses and most of the new siding on the house had melted and the eves were smoldering when the truck arrived. The contractor said it was going to cost too much and take too long to have the garbage hauled away. It seems we never have enough time to do it right, but we always have time to do it over.

One night a lady reported an explosion in her neighbour's back yard. When I arrived, there was no sign of a fire but the lady pointed at the house in question. I rang the doorbell and a man came to the door. As the porch light came on, I asked him if there had been an explosion in his yard and he said no. Now if you have ever seen Wile E. Coyote after one of his Acme bombs goes off in his hands, you'll know what I was looking at. His face was beet red, he had no eyebrows or eyelashes, and his moustache and hair were brown and frizzled. I convinced him to go to the hospital and I got the true story from his wife, it involved wet firewood and a gallon of gasoline.

In the long run, it's safer to recycle. At least that's what McGregor says.

Competition in the Back Yard

A few generations gathered for a brunch on the weekend and as the sun came out for a bit, the younger kids, full of sugar and chocolate, ventured out into the back yard.

These days, when kids go outside it is a lot like bears coming out of hibernation. At first they shield their eyes from the glare of the sun then begin to forage around the yard to see what they can find for entertainment.

One of the adults stuck her nose out the door and pointed out that there was a croquet set up on a shelf. The kids found the cardboard box and emptied out the contents on the lawn. There were no directions but a couple of the older ones had 'sort of' played before so they began discussing the rules, inventing new ones and arguing about the course set up.

The girls were very content to finesse the balls through the hoops while the boys looked for every opportunity to put their foot on one ball and smash their opponent's ball across the yard, under the bushes or careening off the fence.

It's difficult to blame them. Genetics dictate that if you give a male a club and a ball he is going to hit as hard as he can. Most boys never learn the meaning of the words like finesse, grace, delicate, sensitive or poise. Particularly where sports are involved.

The rain shortened the game and they came back inside declaring that the boys had won but they had cheated. It's nice to hear that some things never change, generation after generation.

I recall getting a Summer Play Set one year consisting of a croquet set and a badminton set. It didn't long to set up the poles and the net, mark off a court and soon my brothers and our friends were whacking the plastic birdie back and forth and of course using every opportunity to smash it at an opponent's head.

We had a big back yard that was a baseball diamond, a soccer pitch, a football field and a few times that summer, a large croquet course. By the end of the summer, some of the balls were lost, heads were broken from the mallets from violent use other than playing croquet, and more than one of the metal hoops had been mangled up in Dad's lawn mower resulting in us boys learning much colourful language.

Everybody on our street had a big back yard and a shed full of balls of all shapes and sizes and as soon you could find that little needle that screwed into the bicycle pump and inflate the ball, the game was on.

You can buy a croquet video game advertised as "Just like being outside." Sorry, but nothing even comes close to being outside when you are a kid. Getting wet, getting dirty, making up rules, having a wooden ball bruise your shin, those are all character builders. At least that's what McGregor says.

SUMMER

A Summer Day

Early Morning

Awake before seven, a quick glance outside tells me the dew is already gone. I can wear shorts to water the garden. Feeling the sun dried lawn on my bare feet makes me feel like I'm ten years old again.

The sprinkler mist catches a few rays of early sun and uses the tiny rainbow to remind me that this day is a new beginning. The dribbles of water dripping off the pumpkin leaves create the only sound. Other than that it is just, well, quiet.

I grab a couple of tall weeds and pull them out. The others are small and in among the plants so I'll just leave them for now. Sort of the way we treat our problems. As long as nobody else sees them we ignore them, wait until they are bigger and ugly before we decide to deal with them.

It even smells like summer, dry and dusty. I feel a strong pull to be on my bike, headed to the old wooden Gueho

Bridge to go fishing; but neither the bridge nor the fish are there now.

The dog waits outside the garden gate. She does not come in. Her obedience earns her a biscuit. How she knows I have a day off escapes me and she is anticipating a walk or a ride in the truck, or both. She paces expectantly around the path to the gate.

Of course she loves me. I have never yelled at her about math tests or broken windows, just lots of affectionate pats and small rewards once in a while. I wonder if it's just that easy.

I start toward the back steps and she sits and stares. I please her no end by changing direction for the garage. The garage is where her leash is, and she knows I need the walk as much as she does.

Before Lunch

The car radio plays summer songs that are just right for this morning. They help find a parking spot right in front of the coffee shop, a sure sign that things will keep going right. There, the perfect outdoor table, part sun, part shade. Things grow better in those conditions, even relationships blossom.

I am watching for her through the door, past the tables, the way she usually arrives. Unexpectedly, she approaches from the other direction. Now, I'm not sure if she is radiant because of the sun behind her or is the sun suddenly brighter because of her radiance!? I hold her for just a minute and the all the other stuff just melts away and we seem to be there alone, just her and I.

We share our morning for as long as we can. Then we touch and go, a quick landing and then off again.

After Lunch

My mother and I walk across the hot reflecting blacktop into the church. It's a short sleeve summer funeral to remember an old neighbour. I recognize some of the old farmers, eighty years plus. Past summers, I have hauled their hay and fixed their tires, eaten their roasts and drank their lemonade. But those were long ago July days bent over tractor wheels, under straw hats, raking fields in the dust. The gospel is easily received here, and we learn that the farmer will plant another crop in a place that has no weeds to pull, just perfect soil.

His gracious family smiles and greets us through tear stained make-up. The church ladies hover, refilling the juice and coffee and replenishing the endless trays of crustless sandwiches and Nanaimo bars.

Late Afternoon

Home again. It is still hot so I pull a lawn chair into the shade, close my eyes and imagine a pool back here would be nice. I dive in and open my eyes in the depths to bright reflections, sparkles of sheer delight. Two boys explode into the back yard and the refreshing bubble bursts as I surface.

The two of them are 'gut laughing.' I have no idea what about, probably trouble, but the laughter is healthy and young and just what you need after an old man's funeral.

Their noise conjures a bunch of memories of long ago summer sounds.

Sounds of a game of scrub blend into smells of corn roasts, which soften into Cultus picnics shared by all the families. They fade a bit with each passing summer. It is not easy or safe to re-live your youth and even more difficult to prepare a meal from a lawn chair. I surrender my back yard to the boys.

Evening

In my writing spot, the shade is sundown colored and the sound is just, well, quiet.

The felt pen eagerly anticipates its daily walk and paces expectantly around the blank page. Maybe I'll let it off the leash to run through some rhymes, maybe explore a new path, or both. Maybe I'll just write about today. A day that has passed and unfolded as it was supposed to, whether we actually planned it that way or just thought we did.

Either way, for a summer day, it turned out pretty nice. At least that's what McGregor says.

Not Waiting for Summer

I was watching my grandson play baseball on a recent rare, pleasant afternoon. His little sister was terrorizing other children and her mother and, inevitably, bonked heads with one of the boys, producing a couple of instant goose eggs. In her two and a half short years I have resigned myself to the fact I will be seeing her in bruises and Band-Aids more often than jewelry and make-up. Her Mom consoled her and I offered a grandpa kiss to make it better. She jumped up in my lap for about ten seconds and then was gone again. But she smelled of sunscreen, wisps of strawberry blonde hair whisked my cheek, and her skin was warm. She was summer.

I realized that's what I had been waiting for, some sign or promise that would signal there would be a summer this year. March had been doing a great Hillary Clinton impersonation, just refusing to quit. It brought its blustery winds and bullied right through April. With its cold rain, it had pestered the daylights out of the first few weeks of May, refusing to concede. I wouldn't be surprised to see the TV weatherman predicting the days to come with Cowichan sweaters instead of Hawaiian shirts.

But my granddaughter's quick visit had reminded me what summer was supposed to be. I remembered coconut suntan lotion on a long weekend Penticton beach. I could feel strands of hair on my cheek, blowing in a top down convertible driving home on a hot July night. I could feel the warmth of lifting sleeping kids out of car seats, exhausted after an all-day August picnic.

Whatever chemical imbalance we were suffering from lack of sunshine could surely be overcome by will power, by attitude, by sheer determination that it was June, therefore it should be summer. I decided I would make it so.

I found the sandals in the closet where they were thrown last September. I brought my oscillating fan in from the garage. I turned off the furnace. I put the screens on the patio doors and I dug out my shorts and put a pair on. I dragged my barbecue out of corner, wiped off the dust and fired it up, for no other reason than to smell it burning.

I hosed off my patio and my lawn chairs and hooked my hammock between the fir trees. Tonight, regardless of the weather, I will grill hamburgers, with a huge side of potato salad. I will ignore the neighbours peeking out the windows, ("Hey honey, come look at what he's doing this time!") as they watch me flip burgers while my pasty white arms and legs are covered with goose bumps. I will plop in my Beach Boys 8 track and crank it up, and after dinner, I will drive to Crescent Beach for a maple walnut ice cream cone.

Some people enjoy a pleasant walk in the rain, others complain about how wet they got. Some people see clouds covering the sun; others see the sun peeking through the clouds. Some people believe they should be depressed because they are deprived of vitamin D from lack of ultraviolet light; others wake up with their own special sunshine and let it flow out from them all day.

I am not waiting any longer; my granddaughter felt like summer so I say it starts right now. At least that's what McGregor says.

The First Taste of Summer

One day last week, a young girl brought me a piece of strawberry short cake. A simple volunteer appreciation event had been planned for all those dedicated people who help out at the Douglas Park Community School and the students handed out hand-made thank-you cards, performed a Hip-Hop dance routine and thanked us with punch and dessert.

I'm always amazed at how much you can get back from volunteers for just a t-shirt, a pepperoni pizza and a simple, heartfelt thank-you.

On the paper plate in front of me was shortcake covered with large, fresh sliced strawberries all smothered with whip cream. I took my first bite and just like that, it was summertime. Some tastes or smells or sounds can instantly change the season regardless of the weather.

Sitting outside on the deck with a glass of iced tea is a great summer past time, then add in the music from the ice cream truck as it trundles down the street. I recall one summer when we decided to make homemade ice cream. At first it seemed silly because my Dad was a milkman and he could bring home a brick of Hillside ice cream any time he wanted. On a hot day, Mom would slice the pieces into bowls for dessert and maybe add some canned peaches or blueberries or frozen strawberries picked the summer before.

I do recall making our homemade ice cream to be a messy event, lots of laughing and tasting and because it didn't happen very often I think it was easier to get Dad to bring it home. But it was a family event and it was held in the family kitchen. That's the place you really got to know your family.

Another taste of summer for me is root beer and another experiment comes to mind when we decided to make our own root beer one year. I think Dad had bought a box of bottle caps and a bottle cap press at Gibson's Auction one Thursday and we saved up a bunch of pop bottles. Next, we bought some Hires root beer extract and then began another messy afternoon that involved yeast and syrup and sugar.

The biggest disappointment for us boys was finding out that, after all that work and patience, we would have to wait a couple of weeks while it fermented. Looking at all those bottles, full of that sweet elixir and not being able to pop them open was torture on a hot summer day.

But all I have to do is take one swig of a cold A&W root beer and I'm back in that country kitchen with a bottle of that home brew. It always seems better when you make it yourself.

Trout sizzling in a cast iron frying pan over a campfire beside a Caribou lake is a smell and taste that is unequalled by the world's finest restaurants and is truly a summer memory. Summer is the taste of hot dogs covered in fried onions and relish. The smell of flaming marshmallows followed by children's shouts and screams is truly a summer sight and sound, and don't forget to lather the butter on your corncob.

Another day, I had just had a nice lunch with summer salad and a tall ice tea and I was on my way home when I spotted a young boy on the sidewalk waving a sign beside a church parking lot. The neatly lettered poster advertised, "Ice tea 50 cents, cookies 50 cents."

I like to support young entrepreneurs and whatever fundraisers they are involved with. I buy cookies from Girl Guides, apples from Cadets, chocolate covered almonds from the little girl with teeth missing who rings my doorbell and I always try to have a recycling bag of bottles and cans for the Scouts or Beaver's bottle drives. I figure its good Karma and I have been the Dad who has been involved in these fundraisers in the past so I know the planning and logistics that goes into one of these events.

So I pulled into the parking lot for a glass of ice tea. I noticed there were two boys, about nine years old, dressed in summer uniforms of shorts, t-shirts, running shoes and baseball caps. There was no sophisticated food cart, just a red wagon with a cardboard box and big Thermos jug. Both the boys smiled as I approached and the image they presented with the wagon, the signs, and the grins was worthy of a Norman Rockwell magazine cover. They were happy to see me.

"Mister, you can have a cookie for fifty cents, ice tea for fifty cents…" "Or both for a dollar," his partner chimed in. I asked for a glass of ice tea and as one scrambled to get a Styrofoam cup the other readied the jug. They offered up the cup, I gave them a Toonie and, always being known as a big spender, I said, "Keep the change." There was no apparent cash box and the money went into Number One's pocket, obviously some sort of previous partnership agreement had been reached concerning cash flow.

As we were in a church parking lot, I had made an assumption about where the money was going and I asked, "So what are you guys raising money for?" They exchanged glances and shrugged and Number One said, "Nothing really, we were just so like, really bored so we decided to do this." I could support that. After many summers in the fire service I had seen other results of other bored young boys. Grass fires, brush fires, mischief and vandalism were spawned from idle hands on hot days. Selling lemonade was a great option.

I thanked them and wished them good luck and as I drove away I caught them waving and yelling 'Thanks' in my mirror and I envied the ease of their operation. No one had required them to apply for a business licence, there was no Food Safe requirement, no written contract with the property owner to absolve liabilities or agree to a percentage of the revenue.

They had no overhead other than the wagon and the jug, which somehow I think Number Two supplied. Their inventory was probably contributed at no cost by Mom, whether she knew it or not, and they didn't have to provide a venue access and parking/security plan to the authorities. They just wanted to sell cookies and lemonade on a hot summer day. Good for them.

Lemonade and strawberry short cake, all you have to do is add some cotton candy and mini-donuts from the PNE and your summer menu is complete. Tune up your taste buds, here comes summer. At least that's what McGregor says.

Get A Job!

We are a couple of weeks into summer vacation now and no doubt, many young people are hearing, "Get a job!" I remember those plans to sleep in, to hang around, and to goof off. Hey, it was summer! But, if I didn't get job, work would be found for me.

It was the sixties, peace and love, flowers in your hair, trippin' to San Francisco, who wants to work!? Again, Dad explains very clearly that the only 'wood stock' I will see is the wood that he cuts and that I will be piling. But our neighbour has a construction company and he is building some apartment blocks in Burnaby. He asks if I am working for the summer and if not he needs a labourer.

OK, this is good. Blue jeans, no shirt, hard hat, tool belt, body being bronzed by the sun, muscles toned by lifting and pounding, yes, I'll take it. He says to be ready Saturday morning at six.

He pulls up in his pick-up with two other guys in the cab. "Get in the back and find a place to park your butt!" Wait a minute, in the back, what's that all about?

'The back' is a drafty, homemade, leaking canopy filled with concrete encrusted wheel barrows, extension cords, step ladders, nails, boots, rain gear and tools I don't know the names of. It is dirty and it stinks and the truck is moving before I sit down. It is only a 40 minute drive to where we are going but I have 'parked my butt' on a Skil saw so it seems a lot longer.

We stop at the job site. I get out and I'm standing in muck up to my ankles. "Don't just stand there, load the stuff into the wheel barrows and wheel it over to the saw!" I almost dump the first load and I do dump the second load. It is barely 8:30, I am covered with crap from head to toe and we are between two tall buildings so there will be no 'bronzing sun.' I want to quit and go home. No, to San Francisco, there's going to be a love in there, I've heard that.

Exhausted, I fall asleep on the way home, nested on a cardboard box and a rain jacket.

Every day for the next two months, (except the glorious weekends!) I climb into that truck and head to the job site. I get cut, bruised, yelled at, laughed at and dumped on. I am given nasty nicknames and nasty jobs to do. But I also get some pretty good paycheques, I learn a lot of things about a lot of things and by September, I've made some trips up front in the cab and I'm being called Jim.

I worked for them on weekends after school resumed, and I now had a whole bunch of those "When I was your age..." stories to lay on my kids whenever they asked for money!

But in the end, the money was only part of the value. I learned something that we don't teach young people often enough today. You can't sit in the front seat on the first day, you have you earn your spot in the cab. At least, that's what McGregor says.

A Trip to the PNE

Win a house! Win a car! Yes folks, its PNE time again and anyone who grew up in the Lower Mainland or lived here for a while knows that the PNE is a patch in the quilt of our lives! Everyone has at least one PNE memory, good or bad.

Our family trips started with everyone looking frantically for the gate passes that came with our report cards, I'm sure the organizers knew most of these tickets given out in June would be long gone by August. But as soon as good old Mom found them all, off we went.

The first big event of the day was 'Dad looks for a place to park.' We sat quietly while Dad voiced his opinion about people being ripped off and taken advantage of, but eventually we found reasonable parking and walked a mile and a half to the fair grounds.

"Can we go on the rides?" "No," was the answer, "We're going through the barns first." We had chickens, cows, calves and rabbits at home but somehow, these were different and, we would take in at least one horse show.

Great, now we could go on the rides. Nope, the logger's show was on so we'll watch that, but it's close to the rides so, maybe after that. But no, we're going all the way across the grounds to the Foods building. OK, lots of different meals to choose from, but as usual we had Chinese food. Well, great let's head back to the rides!

Oh yeah, here is the BC Pavilion, let's go in and check out the big relief map of B.C. Yes, Langley is the same place as it was last year, can we go now? Yes, but first we have to stop at the Show Mart Building because our cousin demonstrates Jenn-Air Grill ranges there. I never did see how they worked because she always stopped demonstrating to talk when we came in!

OK, OK, now we're heading to the rides, walking right through the games. Dad says they are all rigged and we shouldn't throw our money away. But every year I come closer to knocking those three bottles down and almost get the ring around the bottle top.

Before we can go on the rides, Mom and Dad want to play bingo, so we have cotton candy or a candy apple, something colourful to throw up. One year, Dad wins a 50-cup coffee maker and forever more it is referred to as 'the coffee maker Dad won at the PNE.' Sort of our family's personal Stanley Cup.

Finally we get to the rides. Spinning, falling, flying, dropping, getting dizzy and getting wet! But in spite of all we've seen or done today, we now feel like we've been at the PNE!

In later years, it was a great place to take your girlfriend and laugh, eat and love like only teenagers can.

I'm going in next week, this is my year to win a house or a car. At least, that's what McGregor says.

Roller Coaster

Clickity clack around the bend,
Giggling up the steep incline;
The bottom drops, the breathing stops
That girlie screaming can't be mine!
Slamming wild into the corner
Seatmate squashed against the car,
Sticky candy-apple fingers
Make indentations in the bar!
Limbs contorting, flailing grasping,
Head facing north but body south,
Upside down now, blood is draining,
Prayers are falling from my mouth!
One last turn, it must be over!
To agree to this was so insane!
Jerking, parking, disembarking,
"Hey, who wants to go again!?"

Jim McGregor

Hiding Spot

A special friend,
A picnic basket,
With chilled red wine
And gourmet cheese;
A secluded spot,
Where the only sound,
Is a whispered promise
On a summer breeze.

Summer Memory

She smelled of sunscreen and summer,
Her skin was warm, toasted brown;
The wind caught wisps of her hair
And tossed them around.

Teasing light through the shadows
Found our spot in the shade,
And added some sparkle
To the memory I'd made.

FORE!

I had the pleasure to golf with some great people in the Greater Langley Chamber of Commerce Tournament recently. The rain stayed away, the sun showed up for a bit and the course at Redwoods was in near perfect shape, which is amazing considering the month we've had.

I will be the first to admit that I am no threat to Tiger or any of his friends but this day proved to be even more of a challenge. As I work for the Chamber on a part time basis it seemed only proper that I not try to show up any of our guests who came to support the event, I didn't want to make anyone feel bad.

It is very difficult to pretend you are a poor golfer. I had to hit the ball in such a way that it merely dribbled off the tee, while the rest of my foursome was whacking it out of sight down the fairway. I purposely hit a few into the bush dejectedly saying, "Darn, I don't know what's wrong today!" If they launched their iron shots high into the sky, I took care to top mine and scoot them along the ground, chasing squirrels into the trees or frogs into the ponds. I putted too short or too long, only to placate my guests, I'm just that kind of guy.

I still took time to cheer my group with at least one snappy golf joke at each hole. They must have been getting tired though, because they didn't seem to laugh at the jokes on the last three holes.

Golf is an interesting game. If you consider that from the time you start your backswing to the time you connect with the ball is 1.5 seconds, and you hit the ball an average of four times a hole for eighteen holes, you are actually only 'golfing' for one minute and forty-eight seconds in an entire round of golf! Now at the risk of sound like a non-golfing wife, girl friend or husband, 'what the hell are you doing out there for five and half hours!?'

Well, golf courses are really pretty. It is an opportunity to sit in an idyllic setting, birds twittering, a slight breeze rustling through the leaves and grasses, watching the water fowl land and take off on the quiet pools and ponds. In between those 1.5 second bursts of adrenalin you have to wait for golfers ahead to get out of danger of your shot, so this is your quiet time. A golfer's family and co-workers will benefit from this calming experience and some personalities have to calm like this three or four times a week.

No one speaks loudly or moves unexpectedly, you maintain the decorum of perfect ladies and gentlemen. It is a chance to bond with new friends. By the time five and half-hours have passed, you know where each one works, what family they have, what hobbies and interests they enjoy. In fact, you probably learn more about a perfect stranger in that afternoon than you know about family or neighbours you have known for years.

The scorecard is not important. It has been time away from noise, phones, and labor and only one minute and forty-eight seconds of frustration.

Some advice for golfers, wear two pair of socks in case you get a hole in one, at least that's what McGregor says.

Bicycles – Summer Transportation

Premier Campbell sent me $100.00 and asked me to go to his Smart Choices website to choose some way to spend it to reduce my carbon footprint. One of the ideas was a new bicycle. Certainly I wouldn't mind replacing my shaky maroon/rust mountain bike with one of those new chrome yellow or fluorescent green ones that whisper by me when I'm out pedaling.

I've never had a fancy bicycle. My first one was my older brother's worn out CCM. There were no frills like hand brakes or chain guards. Once in a while the chain would grab my pant leg and slam me down on the bar. Remember that guys? Boys that wore hats with ear flaps or pants with bicycle clips had a tough time in elementary school and a torn right pant cuff was a badge of courage.

My first new bike was a heavy duty Schwinn with balloon tires and a big black metal paper carrier on the front handlebars. Good for the paper route but not so good for speed, unless you were going downhill. One day and as my buddy and I were coasting down the 208th St. hill, which was mostly gravel back in those days, my jacket was in the carrier and a sleeve worked its way through, jammed between the spokes and the front forks and the bike stopped, right now. I became the Human Cannonball arms stretched out in front, and landed hard. That indentation you can still feel with your right tires near the bottom of the hill, well that was where I landed.

My kids don't like me riding my bike. My daughter chides me to take my cell phone with me so I can call an ambulance and my son is much more comfortable taking the training wheels off his kid's bikes than thinking about me challenging a nature trail or negotiating traffic.

But they both have reason for their concern. They were young children but they still remember the day I tried to avoid a jogger on my bike and hit a telephone pole. I was worried when the doctor told me I had a Grade 3 shoulder separation until my brother pointed out they call it that because it is usually only kids in Grade 3 that run into things with their bikes.

Then there was the late Thursday night at the fire hall, OK, early Friday morning, when I convinced my buddy I was qualified to ride his Honda Six Fifty-four. I did OK until I came into the lot too fast, and the bike and I went separate ways. I could hear the concerned voices of my men as they performed their assessment, but they seemed far away. That's because they were. They were checking out the bike on the other side of the lot, oblivious to my DNA smeared across the asphalt. At times, firefighters can be as mean as elementary school boys.

There were other suggestions on the web site, like running shoes for instance. Well, I paid $100.00 for a 1956 Plymouth once, a whole car, so I'm sure not paying $100.00 for a pair of running shoes. Besides, I stepped in a hole jogging once and tore up my ankle.

So Mr. Premier, if you don't mind I'm just going to fill up my tank with your $100.00.

It will probably be safer for everyone; at least, that's what McGregor says.

Jim McGregor

Work Bees and Picnics

Hot summer days should be approached carefully. Starting early, and moving at a slower pace through the heat of a July day seems to make it last longer, and that's good if you're planning a work bee or a picnic.

A little rental house on our church property in Murrayville was in need of some repair and a coat of paint. The call went out, the paint was bought and the day was set. We started in the cool of the morning and with a seven-man crew this should be done in no time. We assigned scrapers and maskers and trim painters and the day started quietly, then the stories began. There were stories of re-roofing grain elevators in Saskatchewan or a summer painting barns in Alberta. There were stories about building houses or cabins. There were jokes and laughter and the ladies brought muffins and coffee for the morning break and sandwiches and tea for lunch.

The paint went on and what wasn't finished would be completed later in the week. But as it turned out, the day wasn't about painting at all; it was about fellowship and the rewards that come with dirty fingernails and sore muscles at the end of the day. It was chance for some cross generation sharing and a return to what the word neighbour really means. On top of it all, the house looks great.

Later in the week, I was pleased to accompany my Mom to the annual Milner picnic held at another little white church. My first duties as a volunteer firefighter were to respond to the Milner fire hall and take out the old '49 Mercury pumper when the siren sounded. Some of my mentors from those early days were at the picnic and we shared some war stories.

Generations of families arrived and once again the community church became a gathering place and reference point in time as it had for so many years past. Tables kept being added to hold the abundance of food. Nobody thinks of hiring a caterer, it's all pot luck and the fried chicken, sausages, and salads pile up next to thick slices of ham, devilled eggs and a hundred desserts. An accordion and mandolin blend in some old waltzes and the kids line up for the races and the games. It could easily be 1958.

The nametags the people are wearing also appear on the roads and parks of our community. I meet a gentleman whose grandfather carved many of the first local roads with an old bulldozer pulling a grader. Many of these families here today were the first developers of the area. The big difference is that they stayed to fill the churches and schools unlike the numbered companies today that clear land, slap up buildings and disappear.

The old willow tree and a few strategically placed evergreens provide cool shade for gentle conversation. The breeze carries in the smell of fresh cut hay giving legs to more stories. Eddie Jones, a long time area business man, fresh from his hundredth birthday holds court with all who stop by to reminisce, and friends and relatives that haven't seen each other since last year, share pictures and stories. We are encircled by history, memories, neighbours and fellowship; just as a picnic should be.

Work bees and picnics; strength for the body, food for the soul. That's what McGregor says.

Dragon Season

The dragon descended from the cloud cover, extended his wings to get the maximum drag and settled precariously on the ledge between the two mountain peaks. It had been a few years since his last visit and now it was time to burn again. For eons he had been thinning and grooming the forests of the earth; it was a necessary evil.

It was his job to see that the decay covering the forest floor was swept and burned when it got too deep. He was responsible to heat the cones and the pods to the right temperature to split and toss their seeds into the mix of soil and moss. He alone knew which forests must be thinned and which pests destroyed; his task was maintaining balance.

His visits were predicted and expected and yet each time he returned he could see that man was the only creature who had learned nothing from his previous visits. The other residents of the forest instinctively awaited his return. The animals would vacate the area, moving in herds or alone to safer ground. Birds would fly to safety. Anything that could buzz or burrow or slither would seek shelter in the depth of the bark or the darkness of the underground.

Only man would continue to fight the forest fires, each return led to more unnecessary damage and another futile fight, but why?

With a sigh, he cleared his throat and sent a thunderous echo throughout the valley, and then he spat out a tongue of flame. It flashed across the sky and snapped into the dry underbrush and began to smolder, igniting the twigs and grass, which took the fire into the depths of the forest. He watched, then, lifting off his perch he glided into the smoke. With slow, rhythmic beats of his wings, he created currents and spirals in the air that fanned the flames in two directions at once. This one would not be stopped today.

Far below he could hear the shouts of the men and the buzz of their crawling and flying machines, cutting, spraying, and bombing his work. Their useless droplets of water would turn to steam long before they got to the flames. When it was time, the dragon would let the fire go out. Man was never part of the extinguishment.

The heavy smoke obscured the valley floor. It was a mess now, but in the future, the forest would become greener and healthier than before. Only man would suffer loss, nature would prevail.

The dragon settled back on the crag. With a sweep of his wing tip, he gently cleared the snow and dust away from the words that had been long ago etched into the rock face: The Dragon starts the fires, Nature puts them out; man just gets in the way. That's what McGregor says.

Wildfire

Thunder rumbles in the distance,
Gusts of warning wind slip by,
Branches turn to shield their needles,
Lightening splits the summer sky.

Wisps of smoke sneak from the brambles,
Sparks crackle up along the vines;
Scooting up the wick to candle
In a crown of fir and pines.

Timber tumbles down the hillside,
Heat assaults the valley floor;
Blackened, soot-caked devastation,
Then,
Blades of grass appear once more

Campsite Comfort

I was passing through the camping section of a store and a coffee pot caught my eye. It was drip coffee maker for a camp stove! 'Make coffee just like at home,' the box said. Excuse me; camping coffee pours from a blackened pot that sits on the campfire grill all week. Then I saw a complete outdoor kitchen that unfolds into a counter top, a double sink, racks, shelves, and cupboards. 'Bring your kitchen to the campsite' it says. Whatever happened to a plastic basin on the picnic table and a clothesline between two trees?

It got worse. Double air beds with legs and a 'flocked top to keep the sheets from sliding off.' Sheets!? Who takes sheets camping? This bed was designed to fit in a modular tent with three rooms. There were sleeping bags good to -25 C, catalytic heaters, 1100-watt generators, portable hot water heaters and campsite lighting packages and stainless steel double-pronged camping forks. All the comforts of home for your campsite.

The mark of an experienced camper is one who can wake up freezing in the middle of the night, untangle themselves from dozens of sweaty arms and legs, step over four or five snoring bodies and go to the bathroom without waking anyone up. It is not supposed to be like home.

Let me illustrate this. One weekend when summer had stretched into September, a couple of our families went to manning Park. Just adjacent to our campsite were your basic outdoor toilets. One evening, just at dusk, someone entered one carrying a disposable Bic flashlight. For those of you who aren't familiar with these, there are now billions of these colourful plastic lights lying in landfills across North America.

They dropped their light down the hole; it stuck in the muck with the light glowing upwards into the outhouse. As the evening darkened this became a very ethereal sight. Now it was not as spectacular as an image of the Virgin Mary appearing on a pressure washed Maritime Tim Horton's but it did create quite a pilgrimage. People came from all over the campsite to see the "glowlet", the "shiny john" the "lighthouse", and other names I can't print here. Families stopped on their way back from the ranger's talk at the amphitheatre. Tourists took pictures of the unearthly scene as if a UFO had landed.

My brother in law sketched a bracket design on a napkin and, as another shot of rum was added to the coffee, we added up the outhouses, times parks, times brackets, and envisioned millions of dollars in the outhouse illumination business. Why had no one thought of this before?

Eventually, a voice shook the night, "Who's the jerk who dumped on the flashlight!?" We all turned in slow motion and, sure enough the glow was gone. Someone would have to change these lights regularly, wouldn't they? The napkin was tossed into the flames and we watched our Freedom 55 plans literally go up in smoke.

Outhouses at campsites are not supposed to be lit. You are supposed to try finding them with a flashlight that cuts out as you approach roots or rocks on the path, or when you hear a rustle in the bush or search for the toilet paper.

It is not natural to turn a campsite into a condominium and, you don't need an 1100-watt generator to see the stars. That's what McGregor says.

The Long Weekend

The long weekend is closer than it appears. I'm sure many fathers that have campsites reserved are checking the long-range forecast. As Friday, Saturday and Sunday pop up on the screen they pray to see that little yellow sun icon, even just a portion of it.

Long weekends seem to start earlier now. The traffic builds on Thursday afternoon as more people take that extra day they have saved. Any jump on the masses is a good one. Even if it just means getting the lawns cut at home, gardens watered and leaving the place neat and tidy. I've never quite figured that out. We leave our place looking great so we can head off to a gravel campsite in an overgrown campground. We leave a quiet street to merge in with the lemming-like weekend trek, honking, braking, swerving, and cursing.

Your back yard will sit unmolested, weeds gone, grass trimmed, and patio furniture neatly arranged on the solid, flat deck. Hot tub water is circulating quietly and the propane barbecue is covered in the corner. That sounds like a nice place to spend the weekend.

115

But, you are going camping. A couple of bathroom stops, a lunch at a restaurant that costs half of what you planned to spend this weekend, and you have arrived. You wait patiently for the couple in the next campsite to back their trailer in. After a minute or two, you decide to save their marriage and you ask the missus if she would like you give the back-up directions. You make two new friends.

Your kids and wife have disappeared and so you set up the camp. It crosses your mind that Hannibal crossed the Alps with less than what you have brought along for three days.

After you have put up the tent, levelled the motor home or rolled out the rooms of your fifth wheel, you go for a walk. At home, the remote control for the TV enjoys a much-needed rest on the soft arm of your comfortable recliner and all the World Cup games are being played in spite of your absence. You try to block this out of your mind as you sit, holding your breath in an outhouse.

Next, you explain why you are not driving back to the pizza place you passed on the way in. The hamburger patties may be a bit pink in the middle but they are certainly done on the outside, there is nothing wrong with them, that's dinner, eat it or go hungry.

You make a coffee and go for another walk, until you feel the raindrops and you have to go back and put up a tarp. It will look less like a homeless camp if you hang a Canadian flag from the pole.

But years later, the family will remember those weekends more than any spent at home. Forget the long range forecast, go, it's the long weekend. At least that's what McGregor says.

Camping Not Like the Brochures

The gas prices are back up and the forecast is for unsettled weather with below normal temperatures. These two facts combined must mean we have a long weekend approaching. I haven't been away on a long weekend for a quite a while; my backyard has a place to recline and read and another to sit and write. My camping days are behind me, and my Brookswood campsite with indoor plumbing and a comfortable bed seems to suit me better these days.

I like to look at the ads put out by Tourism B.C. or the articles in the Beautiful B.C magazines. You know the ones I mean. The couple sitting in their camping chairs drinking coffee beside a perfect campfire in an isolated camping spot, the sun setting on a placid lake, the red canoe pulled up on shore; 'that's what I miss,' you say to yourself.

Those spots do exist in B.C., hundreds of them and you can reserve them. The only control you don't have is your choice of neighbours. Shortly after you get set up and sit down to enjoy the view, smell the pine and feel the sun on your face, an old truck and camper pulls into the site next to you. From the stickers pasted all over it, it is obvious they have been campers for a long time. The trailer towed behind is loaded to the top.

At least four kids tumble out and Mom gets out holding a crying baby. Dad starts yelling instructions and tents go up, tarps and ropes appear and cover the site with such speed and precision that surely these people are long lost descendants of circus folk. The man comes over holding one of the biggest coffee travel mugs you have ever seen and plunks down in your site and becomes your new best friend for the weekend.

The sound of a diesel engine interrupts your new friend's theory on global warming and you look up to see a Greyhound sized motor home mooring next door. It blocks out the sun on your face. Hydraulics start to hum as the machine levels itself, spits out bedrooms and kitchens and transforms into a home away from home. An old fella in Bermuda shorts and black socks and sandals waves as he exits followed by his wife in a large Hawaiian print dress holding a little dog. Everyone exchanges hellos and their satellite goes up and their generator comes on.

Across the road is a double campsite that only had a small tent in place when you arrived. As the afternoon wears on, a 4x4 pulls in with dirt bikes strapped in the box, the van full of teens arrives around dinnertime and the final spot is taken up by an old VW bus. The driver of the bus has long shaggy hair and, you guessed it, as soon as it gets dark he brings out a guitar.

As the evening draws to a close, you have missed the sunset, the baby won't stop crying and the little dog is barking at 'Bye, Bye, Miss American Pie' coming from across the road. The bus people are watching a DVD and your new best friend and his kids are roasting marshmallows on your campfire. You haven't seen your wife for three hours.

Camping was never like the brochure, but I'm glad I have the memories. At least that's what McGregor says

Back Yard Camping is the Best

I noticed a tent go up in the back yard at one of the neighbours last weekend. Back yard camping is always the best for lots of reasons. Carrying the tent and sleeping bags fifty feet from the basement doesn't give anyone a chance to ask, "Are we there yet?"

In the light of the day with no shadows, evidence of ghosts or any sign of nocturnal critters, the kids want the tent as far away from the house as possible. No sense camping out if you can see your bedroom window.

Mom and Dad want the tent in a spot that can be seen from the kitchen window or the deck. Not exactly a guard tower but the premise is the same, they want to know what is going on at all times.

Once the sleeping bags and air mattresses are in place and the comic books, flash lights and stuffed animals are brought in, it looks like home away from home and the excitement builds as the evening approaches. The kids strategize about who will sleep where and plot schemes to stay awake all night.

But the campsite is ready. No 300Km drive in heavy traffic, no noisy camping neighbours and all the amenities of home.

The bathroom, for instance. Being able to walk from the tent to a hot shower and flush toilet is pretty darn good. I want you all to close your eyes for a second and let your olfactory senses take you into one of those campsite outhouses. Paper on the floor, wet toilet seats, gagging odours, and bugs all around.

During the day, the biggest flies buzz constantly around your head and in the dark of the night they give way to the hungriest mosquitoes who know just exactly how vulnerable you are and how difficult it is to pee, hold a flash light and swat at the same time. Brushing teeth in your own bathroom should never be taken for granted.

Once the bathroom chores are done, it's time to settle in the tent. Now, in the dark, under the shadows of the tall trees, the kids notice how far away from the house they have put the tent. Barking dogs two blocks away sound like wolves in their own back yard. Birds taking off though the trees must be vampire bats and the squirrel running along the fence is surely a cougar, if not a bear. Is this even the same back yard?

Eventually the question is asked, "Dad, are you going to sleep out here with us tonight?"

The proximity of the kitchen is great too. Once the kids have dozed off after pleading then threatening, you can sneak in to the house, turn on the electric lights and make a cup of coffee. After all, even if the kids do fall asleep, Mom and Dad will keep one ear pointed to the back yard in case of emergencies. It is usually a long night.

About three in the morning when the evening has finally cooled down, it's not uncommon to hear small footsteps on the stairs and find a couple of back yard campers, holding their teddies, wrapped in blankets and head for their bedrooms. "It got too cold Mom."

But the next day bigger plans are hatched for the night to come. After all, cougars in your campsite is something to brag about. At least that's what McGregor says

Cooling Off

The little girl in the convenience store looked like a rainbow Popsicle. Her cool sundress was purple, red and yellow, her flip-flops were bright green and a big blue barrette struggled to contain wisps of blonde hair. I was envious of her on this ninety degree day as I stood in line in my scratchy slacks, dress shoes and sports jacket. Then she announced to everyone that she was getting a Slurpee and going to the water park! Now I was downright jealous.

I closed my eyes and went to those cooling off spots I used to go to on a hot summer day when I was kid; I ran full speed and dove in. Take a second and do that yourself right now! We didn't have water parks or recreation centers. There was no way you could run through the sprinkler if you were on a well. Any extra water was for the vegetable garden and if the cistern level dropped below the pump, that meant a call to Ed Deglan for a truckload of water. It wasn't for playing with.

But across Glover road behind Thatcher's farm, the stream widened into a pool wide enough to swim across and

124

deep enough to cannon ball into. The banks were clay and the bottom was mucky so we could only swim until the water got too murky. But it was cold and refreshing.

There was also the occasional trip to Aldergrove Beach. This huge man-made lake is now the Aldergrove Lake Regional Park but it was once just a big pool of water in the middle of a field. A four inch supply pipe in the middle gushed ice cold water five or six feet high in an endless spout and the dare was to swim out to it and let the frigid stream cascade down on top of you. It was a great picnic spot. Does anyone remember the Saturday midnight swim at the Aldergrove Beach Rock Festival? That event was held forty years ago last month.

Longer day trips took us to Cultus or Allouette Lakes where races down the docks ended up in the mountain fed lakes, taking your breath away when you hit the water. A weekend or more could mean a Penticton campsite with hot sand and warm Okanogan swimming.

Raising my own children, we were fortunate to have pools and recreation centers and we also had city water so the water fights and the sprinkler chases were all part of the summer. I recall a birthday when we had purchased a terrible device called a 'Slip and Slide'. I set it up and decided to cool off and make sure the thing was safe at the same time. I took three strides and landed on my back and head. They set me in the shade and carried on with the party.

At a family reunion at my parent's hometown, Dad was standing at twilight with a coffee, eyes straining out over Picnic Lake. I asked him what he was looking at and he replied that he used to stand on this spot and watch his brother swim across the lake, making sure he was OK. Everyone has a special memory of their 'old swimming hole.'

I'm finished writing and it's still hot. Hmmm, a Slurpee at the water park, eh. That just might be the answer. At least that's what McGregor says.

Heat Wave

Knee deep in January snow, we longed for summer. Drenched by ten days of March rain we begged for the warmth of July. Well folks, it's here and we're still complaining. Half the province is burning and the rest is baking or frying and we are actually hoping for some cool rainy days.

The people of the Fraser Valley do not like extremes. We want the temperature to stay between and 10 and 25C all year round. We want to keep one nylon jacket at our back door that we can wear every day. We want to have the same weight of blankets on our beds in July that we have in January. We don't mind a bit of snow shovelling or sunburn but we are not that in to standing in line for snow blowers or air conditioners. Just keep the weather simple, thank-you.

The first couple of days of oppressive heat were interesting, a conversation topic. By the third day, no one was having fun anymore. Fashion sense goes out the window. No one coordinates outfits by the third day. Striped tops with plaid shorts, clothes you haven't worn for years, whatever is clean and dry becomes the dress of the day, nobody's doing laundry. Stained armpits are everywhere, but no one cares what anyone looks like. Even some of the diehards take their socks off and just wear sandals.

Tempers are short; drivers growl and snarl their way through traffic. The ones with air conditioning don't want to get out of their vehicles, but they know they'll look pretty dumb sitting in the driveway with the car running. The car that doesn't have air conditioning is recognizable by the sweaty driver and the kids that travel like spaniels with their heads out the windows, ears and hair flapping in the thick, warm air.

Bags of ice are sought after like bags of salt were six months ago. I overhear a shopkeeper tell a customer his supplier is unable to keep up with the demand. How can you run out of ice, did someone forget the recipe or something? It's frozen water in a plastic bag! But, I'm sure it will be a good reason to raise the price a buck or two.

People that buy the heat pumps or air conditioners make sure everyone else knows they have one. They work it into the conversation or they stand behind closed windows with fancy drinks and look out with contempt on the staggering masses, oblivious to their cries, "I'm melting, I'm melting!" My son asked if we were getting an air conditioner. I told him honestly no, that if I got one he may never want to leave. I read recently that the human species is the only one on earth that allows their offspring to move back home. The secret is to keep the den hot and uncomfortable.

Then there are the people with 'The Pool.' Did you notice how much they enjoy saying things like, "It was sure nice to jump into 'The Pool' when I got home," or, "Even the water in 'The Pool' was warm last night." I try not to be shallow, but it's enough to make you go off the deep end.

Hang in there and chill out brothers and sisters, it's only a couple of weeks 'til the PNE, we'll have rain by then for sure. At least that's what McGregor says.

Jim McGregor

Getting Away

I got out of town for a couple of days this week and renewed some old acquaintances in Penticton. As a bonus I also got to sit awhile and feel that wonderful hot Okanagan sun on my face. A couple of bright, warm days back to back can do wonders for your disposition.

For me, it never seems like my holiday begins until I pass Hope. This trip was no different as the rain tapered off as we approached town and the wipers were off soon after I hit the Hope-Princeton. No doubt there is some geographical or meteorological explanation for it but it always seems to be cloudy and wet when you come through the tunnel in Yale or round the bend at the Coquihalla Junction and you know your vacation has ended.

I hadn't been on the Hope-Princeton for many years; the wide-double lanes and graceful sweeping curves of the Coquihalla and its connectors have spoiled us all, and we have become more focused on the destination rather than the journey.

130

Before that super slab was carved through the wilderness, we had the Hope-Princeton or the Canyon routes to choose from and if you happened to get behind a big rig at the old Alexandria Bridge in the Canyon or at Britannia Mines outside of Princeton, there was nowhere to pass for miles and as a passenger you became familiar with the scenery.

As a small boy we made many trips along those routes headed for camping or fishing holidays and as I drove up this time many memories came back. Not far out of Hope is the famous Hope Slide. If you're lucky, the clouds have disappeared and you can see the section of Johnson Peak that let go in April of 1965. For a few years after that, the slide was a place where we took visitors. Mom would pack up a thermos of coffee and make some sandwiches and we would make a day of it. I still marvel at the job the Army Engineers did in carving a temporary road over that mess. We still travel over it today.

Just before Manning Park is a large pullout/rest stop. There is nothing there today but when I was a ten-year-old boy, that was a place to stop and see the giant wooden cigarette hanging from a noose. Next to it was a sign that said, "He who threw this should also be hanged!" Behind the sign was the very dramatic scene of a burned out hillside. Black scorched earth and twisted trunks and fallen pine trees, the result of a massive forest fire started by a single cigarette. It was a stark message when we were told it would take over fifty years to grow back.

As I drove past the beautiful, thick green forest this trip I realized it was indeed fifty years since I had first seen that sign and now the reclamation was almost complete. Nature just shakes her head, rolls up her sleeves and patiently goes about covering up our scars, time after time. As beautiful as it is now, somehow I think that cigarette should still be hanging there as a reminder.

If you have vacation time coming, use it, use it all. Get some rest for yourselves and make some memories for your children, fifty years goes by pretty fast. At least that's what McGregor says.

Hide Outs

I was travelling along a back road on a not quite summer day recently when I was surprised by two young boys bursting out of the bush and scurrying across the road. They were about ten or eleven, wearing t-shirts and shorts and scampering into the ditch in their bare feet. I was reminded of a neighbour who used to tell us that he was one of four brothers and his Dad used to tell the neighbours if they saw his boys running through their yards they were to stop them and kick them in the butt because they were either on the way to trouble to coming from it.

The taller boy vaulted the fence post into the field and the smaller one squeezed through the strands of barbed wire and caught up just as they disappeared into the bush. They only thing they left behind were a thousand memories.

I could feel the grass and stubble between my toes, running bare foot on feet that had soles as thick as leather by the time summer was over. No doubt, the boys were headed for a fort or some covert place of refuge that was off limits to parents, teachers, bullies, bosses, and babes.

I recalled such a place in the bush between Mufford Crescent and Norris road. Hidden in the thick bush was a cave carved out of the dense blackberry vines. You had to crawl into it and the floor was lined with cardboard and a scattering of comic books and baseball cards. It was cool on those August days and the bush above it was enough to keep it dry when it rained. The dog would know exactly where we were headed and she would charge around chasing rabbits until she collapsed, covered with brambles panting on the cardboard. Little brothers were allowed in but never on their own, and once chores were done it was our private place to hang out.

I put up a play house for my youngest son and I have a picture of two three year old boys leaning out the window with a sign, 'No Girls Allowed' nailed to the wall above the ladder. The sign eventually fell off but when he turned fifteen I put it back up for my own peace of mind. Tree houses and forts were great places to go to talk without being heard or to laugh as loud as you wanted. They were secret sharing spots and secluded thinking rooms.

We still have our own forts today. Maybe it's the shop in the garage or the basement. Maybe it's the weekly meeting of the service club you belong to or the place where old cars gather in the parking lot. Maybe it's the sewing room or the gazebo in the garden. Perhaps it's the room with the old stereo where you go when you feel like writing.

Regardless of where it is or how often you go there it serves the same purpose as the old fort did. It's the place where there are no bosses or customers, no employee meetings or training sessions, just a place to talk, or listen or laugh or think.

If don't have your special hiding spot yet, make one this summer and go there bare foot as often as you can, but don't give the secret password to too many people. At least that's what McGregor says.

Summer Nutrition

I was watching a Nutritionist on the news last weekend. A Nutritionist specializes in advising us what to eat, when to eat it, what quantities we should be consuming and what is bad or good for our bodies. I'm pretty sure we used to call that type of expert a mother.

The focus of this lady's presentation was the summer barbecue and how easy it is to stray off a diet during the summer months when our routines have changed. Travelling, visiting, partying are all disruptive to what she refers to as a "safe nutritional regimen".

Personally, I am eating much better than I have in the past following the adage, 'too soon old, too late smart.' I by no means follow a safe, nutritional regimen but I'm pretty healthy these days. But when I get invited out to a barbecue or a picnic, I reward myself by disrupting my routine or, "pigging out" may be a more appropriate phrase.

Our expert had two plates of food in front of her. One had a steak, some potato salad, macaroni salad and some potato chips, about 1600 calories on that plate. The other plate had some green salad, some noodle stuff, and some raw vegetables, less than 500 calories. Her point was that the food on both plates was on the buffet table and all it took was some discipline to choose the lighter fare.

Okay folks, we're at a barbecue, the sun is shining, people laughing, music, liquor and a table spread with all manner of delicacies and she recommends we practice restraint. A fellow ahead of me in a buffet line passed up all the green salads explaining that salad is not food, salad is what your food eats before it goes to the butcher. You don't take up a lot of valuable space on your plate with salad.

She pointed out that, if you are going to eat a steak to choose a small cut with no bone because there is a high fatty content between the meat and the bone, which is not good for you. I think she is referring to that strip that bubbles and sizzles and explodes in your mouth, the true essence of eating meat. Eating a steak without a bone is like having a football team without a quarterback, but don't get me started on that.

Corn on the cob she tells us should be steamed so we don't boil out the nutrients and of course stay away from the butter and salt. Sorry ma'am but when you finish a cob of corn there should be bits of corn on the front of your shirt and butter dripping from your chin.

She showed us some diced potatoes with some sort of sissy low calorie drizzle on them, not for me. I will choose that big Idaho spud, split it down the middle fill it with butter, sour cream, bacon bits, and whatever else I can squeeze in.

Then she says that we should have some exercise, a short walk maybe," Don't forget 100 calories equals 1 mile." She advises we will feel better physically and mentally. I have no intentions of walking to Chilliwack and back and I feel just great, physically and mentally, plopping on my couch, undoing my belt and dozing until someone wakes me up for bed.

That's why it's called the good old summer time. At least that's what McGregor says.

Summer Lawns

From my sun deck, I can gaze over the golden wasteland of my dry dusty back yard. There has been no sprinkling of any kind this summer and only a few faint streaks of green are visible over the septic field or bordering the gardens.

The back yard is well used either by teenagers producing idiotic You Tube videos I don't want see or grandkids piling off and on the trampoline. Baseballs and soccer balls are tossed or kicked around and never put away and plastic jeeps and toys are encroaching into the flowerbeds and bikes are languishing against the trees.

My front lawn has surrendered to the moss again. Three times in seventeen years I have killed the moss, hauled in soil and sand and produced a well-manicured putting green only to watch the moss return the following year.

With the last couple of dry summers I'm surprised we haven't had people around selling lawn insurance like they offer crop insurance in the prairies. I would like be standing in my back yard in late August and have an adjuster saying, "Yep, that's dead all right, here's a cheque for $2500.00."

Dad always said that the front lawn is for the neighbours and the back yard is for the family. We always had a field for football or a rough baseball diamond carved out in such a way that the touchdowns didn't land in the pumpkins and the fly balls stayed out of the corn. When we first moved in there was a row of two foot high fir trees planted and staked at each side of the yard. They were a pain in the butt for rambunctious boys and we were told not to disturb them under any circumstances.

Thirty-five years later they were fifty-foot sentinels protecting the property from wind and snow. They had grown straight and tall and provided a lesson to those boys. If you plan ahead, keep things free from weeds and pests, make sure they are growing in the direction you had planned, they can provide support and protection when you need them the most. That works for kids as well as trees.

I'm not concerned about the drought conditions in my back yard. I am certain that by mid-October, after a couple of weeks of rain, the lawn will be thick and green again and ready to brave the winter. Meanwhile, I'll sacrifice the green grass for the noise and activity. At least that's what McGregor says.

Better Home and Garden

We plant the bulbs and seed the lawn
To see what Nature brings,
But trucks and balls and trampolines
Bloom freely, every spring!

You've seen the picture in the magazine,
That shows a lush green lawn;
It stays that way on a summer day
If you don't let children on.

I like seeing worn base paths,
Carved between the weeds,
So grandkids learn the secrets
Of blowing dandelion seeds.

Some say planting fine azaleas
Makes such perfect garden sense,
But they hinder my dog's digging,
Hiding bones along the fence.

A quiet garden is the perfect place
To hear God's word, they say,
But I've heard Him laugh in my back yard
Listening to my children play.

Summer Storms

I had my grandkids overnight on the weekend. I don't do that enough but then we're all too busy aren't we, too much going on. I often think about how many times I coulda, shoulda, woulda visited people who are gone now, but I didn't. Excuses are like Kleenex, you pull one out and another one pops up waiting to be used.

It was crappy weather so we didn't get to do all the normal outside stuff we normally do but we had a pretty good time and our day was easy.

Just about bedtime the thunder started. We all know that thunderstorms here usually pass over pretty quick but this one looked like it was settling in. We turned off all the lights and sat in the dark in the living room and watched the show outside.

We had some pretty serious discussions about thunder and lightning and my grandson seems to a bit of an expert on mythical gods. I made a joke about Thor getting that name when he dropped his big hammer on his toe and shouted "ouch, I'm Thor." He didn't laugh. Very seriously he advised,

"Grandpa, with all this lightning outside, it's probably not a good time to be making jokes about the gods."

"I'm not scared," his little sister says. But her eyes are just visible above her favourite blanket and she's clutching her stuffed animal very close. I make a feeble Grade Nine science effort to try to explain about positive electrons and high and low barometric pressures but no one is buying it and my lesson plan fades in the next rumble of thunder.

I told them about my Grandma and the little rhyme she taught us to recite during a thunder storm, "The thunder rolled, the lightning flashed, the world was all a shaken; the little pig turned up his tail, and ran to save his bacon." That led to sharing other lightning stories and I related the one about Ben Franklin and the kite and electricity. My granddaughter offers her opinion that Ben probably shouldn't have been outside during the storm. I never really thought about the safety aspect of his scientific breakthrough before.

As the storm rolled over I recalled Okanagan thunderstorms that drenched the tent, collapsed the tarp and flooded the campsite. I remembered sitting outside my uncle's cabin on Turtle Lake Saskatchewan under the stars and the moon and watching a fierce prairie electrical storm travel along the other side of the lake. I thought about previous years' forest fire headlines and how this year the province's underbrush is wetter than Cultus Lake firewood. This storm wouldn't set many fires.

We listened to the rain and hail pelt down on the roof and the sidewalk and the little one says, "I'm not really scared but I think we should turn the lights back on now."

The thunder moves up the valley, everyone gets tucked in and suddenly you realize it is completely quiet. The sky is still, the rain has stopped and the kids are asleep. It reminds me of a time we got caught in a Tofino thunderstorm while hiking and only noticed the rain had quit when we realized how silent the forest had become.

Storms always pass, even the ones we create. The secret is to make the best use of the calm in between them. At least that's what McGregor says.

Going for Fruit

A friend mentioned that she was going to buy some fruit. That caught my attention followed some disappointment when I found out she was just going up the hill to get it locally.

There is nothing wrong with going to a local market but her comment had conjured up the good old days when Mom would announce we were going to Keromeos to get peaches. That was like a mini vacation, even if it was just a day away it was away from the barn, the wood box, the chickens and chores in general.

Dad would spend some time getting the car ready over the next few days. Maybe Jock Fraser would change the oil and grease it up or maybe it was just a general radiator, fan belt, spare tire check. Either way, the canvas water bag would be draped over the hood ornament, Dad would complain about the price of a full tank of gas and the car would be ready.

Because the old Trans-Canada Highway to Hope had nothing like a McDonalds or an A& W, Mom would pack sandwiches, cold chicken, Kool-Aid and, make sure we all went to the bathroom one more time.

Dad didn't like noise in the car. Singing or arguing would distract him from driving and listening for a piston to come through the block or a wheel to fly off. He was always sure something was going to happen and it rarely ever did. But we were quiet and he was ready for anything with one eye on the road and the other on the gauges.

If the Hope-Princeton wasn't busy and we were making good time, we might pull off at a creek for a quick dip in the frigid mountain water. It was good to cool off as our car had what was known as two-forty air conditioning; roll down two windows and drive a forty miles an hour. After Dad had some tea from his big plaid Thermos and we had a snack we were off again.

When we finally got to Keromeos there was always a loud debate about which fruit stand we bought at last year and finally we would settle on one. The hot wind was always blowing and the cold pop and cider always looked tempting. But they were not in the budget.

We loaded the trunk with peaches, nectarines and whatever else was in season. If relatives had heard we were going, often we brought back some for them as well. We brought back cherries for canning and some in a bag to eat on the way home. Our big sister doled them out like gold nuggets so we wouldn't 'get the runs before Hope.'

If the price of fruit had been right maybe we stopped in Hope for dinner at a restaurant and it was always dark when we got home. The next day the stove was fired up, the canners and the jars and the rubber rings were put into an assembly line and the fresh fruit was sealed away.

Then, on a damp, rainy November night after a dinner of stew and dumplings, one of those golden jars would appear on the table, maybe with some ice cream and you could feel that hot Okanagan wind warm up the kitchen. Food tastes so much better when you've worked for it. At least that's what McGregor says.

Food just tastes so much better when you've worked for it. At least that's what McGregor says.

Dog Days of Summer

This summertime column comes with a warning to the faint of heart. It may contain some immature subject matter that is offensive to some readers. It does, however, concern a subject that has at one time affected each one of us and today I discuss how our attitudes have changed over the years.

The inspiration came on a recent summer morning when I was stopped at a red light. Two young boys were running along the shoulder of the road and one had a dog on a leash. Suddenly the dog stopped to do what dogs do when being exercised and one of the boys called, "Dylan, wait I have to pick up the poop." He took the bag out of his pocket and as he has been taught, cleaned up the mess and they were on their way.

Now to all of you of my age, think about us young boys running across the field to play scrub or heading for the fishing hole and suddenly one of the group yells, "Hey guys wait, Patches just pooped and I have to pick it up." Can you even begin to imagine what he would have heard from the rest of the gang!?

I really don't know what happened to all of the dog poop of my youth, knowing it never got picked up. As a matter of fact, it was quite often a source of entertainment. "Hey guys, Larry just stepped in dog poop, way to go Larry!" For the rest of day or even longer he would be 'Dog Poop Larry" and probably stayed that way until Ricky caught his pant leg in the bike chain and then we could make fun of him.

Of course there were the unexpected discoveries. Picture a warm spring morning in class and we have just sung Oh Canada and recited the Lord's Prayer. Kids start sniffing and giggling and when the teacher asks what is wrong she hears, "Miss Smith, someone stepped in dog poop and it really stinks." Then Miss Smith would have everyone check the bottoms of their shoes and eventually the source of the odour would be uncovered.

The offender would be sent from the class to clean it off. For the girls this was not really a problem as penny loafers or saddle shoes were smooth and easy to clean. But every boy learns at eight years old that you cannot clean dog poop from the sole of a sneaker.

Even NASA has not developed a tool that will clean all the little squiggles and designs. Small sticks or paper towels available in school washrooms were never effective and if the janitor caught you running your shoe under the tap there was hell to pay.

I'm sure today our schools have procedures in place so that a student's self-esteem is not damaged. No doubt every teacher's handbook has Section 4A – *A policy and procedure for removing canine excrement from adolescent footwear while maintaining the student's dignity.*

The running shoes finally got completely cleaned that evening when, after everyone was in bed, Mom could smell something amiss and using elbow grease and a Magic Mom Brush, the shoe was thoroughly cleaned and saved for another run through the park.

We all step in some kind of mess from time to time. Learning how to clean it up ourselves is the important part of the lesson. At least that's what McGregor says.

An Honest Day's Work

The impatient lady in the foreign convertible was so close I couldn't see her headlights. I pulled over on the narrow shoulder and let her pass. It was a safe move because I had been driving and daydreaming, a practice I'm sure my insurance people frown upon.

I got out of the truck to watch the farmer pull his round baler across the wide expanse of cut hay. The machine gobbled it up, swallowed it, chewed it, wrapped it in plastic and bounced the round bale back on the ground. One man and one machine clearing the field.

His huge, bright blue, multi-tasking contraption is a far cry from the little grey Fordsons that used to pull the hay rake or the red and white Massey-Fergusons that dragged the baler back when I was a kid.

It had been an uncommonly wet spring and finally a few days of sunshine had been promised, and as the old saying goes, 'make hay while the sun shines.' This first cut was probably for feed for the dairy herd. The plastic wrapped bales would be conveniently stacked close to the dairy barn.

The second cut would likely produce four or five thousand bales from a field this size and that would be for the horses or maybe to sale. That's when a crew would be needed.

I used to look forward to those calls, when a farmer was putting together a haying crew. Some of the big farms would need you for three or four days, other calls would come from a smaller operation and might give you one day of work. Either way, you never turned the call the down if you were available. Sitting at home doing nothing on a summer day was just not acceptable.

When you got to the farm you headed out with the crew, other boys you knew, neighbouring farmers, sometimes a fella 'just passing through' looking for some cash. If you knew the field you stuck to the group that was pulling bales from the level ground. The lower areas tended to produce bales a little heavier. That made a big difference at the end of the day.

For a while, it was like ballet. Walking beside the truck or wagon you could toss up a bale and grab the next one all in one motion. Eventually though, the load got higher and the men were separated from the boys pretty quick. Your swing would have to be timed with the grab of the stacker or it might result in a broken bale back on the ground and worse, a stream of verbal abuse from the rest of your crew. Stacking was an art, each bale locking in the next one. A rickety wooden field bridge or a sharp turn could spell disaster for a poorly stacked load.

The ride back to the barn might be in the fresh air on top of the load or jammed into the dusty cab of a Fargo flat deck. You earned your place in the cab and if you were quiet the ride back to the barn was always educational.

The smell of sweaty bodies mixed with the sun warmed leather seats as you squeezed in between the driver and another farmhand. Some trips, the lessons were taught in silence as the cool air whipped in through the open windows. The faded letters on the time worn gear shift knob spoke volumes about the generations of this family that had hauled this load so many times in past years.

On other trips the farmer might share his philosophy on farming, hay cutting and life as he negotiated the twists and turns of the narrow country roads. His conversations were essays for young men. They were stories about the value of hard work and handshake deals made with honest folks. They were dialogues about the marketing boards and bankers or rants about lawyers and politicians. As tempting as it was to doze off, you were always polite enough to listen and nod, anticipating the meal waiting back at the farmhouse.

Often, the afternoon meal was a roast with all the fixin's. I have had some pretty expensive prime rib dinners in my life but nothing tastes better than a slice of beef you have actually earned. Other times you might be treated to juicy ham sandwiches or a thick slice of fresh bread dripping with honey from the farmer's hives. Pie and ice cream served by pretty farmers' daughters made it a perfect meal. We worked like beggars and ate like kings.

Putting the hay in the loft could be a challenge depending on where you stood in the pecking order. You might get the fun job of feeding the elevator, out in the cool shade of the barn, or maybe you were stuck in the musty, dusty loft.

Up there, every second step you took went between the bales and you had to struggle to keep up as the bales popped through the loft door. If you got behind and a bale fell to the ground, a string of shouts from the rest of the crew would come from below and you found another gear and worked a little harder. It would take three or four glasses of ice tea or lemonade to dissolve the clog building in your throat.

Late in the day, a wisp of breeze would cause everyone to cast a wary glance at the western sky, that's where the clouds would form. Then, the farmer's intuition, coupled with the noon Country Radio Farm Report, would decide the course of action. Like a General addressing the troops before battle he would announce, "OK boys, we're going to pull another load before dark." Then we would be back in the field in the dim light of the cool evening air, the high beams of the trucks and tractors searching for those last few stray bales.

The day ended with a handshake and a cheque or wad of bills that were folded and stuffed into the pocket of your jeans. But the best pay would come if the farmer said, "I'll be giving you a call when we need you again." Then it was home to a shower and "dead in bed" in case the phone rang early in the morning. The blisters, sunburn, sore back and aching arms were badges awarded for a job well done.

Today, the farmer smiles and waves at me as he leaves his field. It looks like someone has dropped huge marshmallows from the sky as the big round white bales wait to be picked up, by another machine. He has single-handedly finished a job in a couple of hours that once took crew of strong young men a day to complete. I don't know if that's progress or not.

I look up at the blue summer sky, smell the cut field and shake my head as I think of all the teenage boys at home in their basements, glued to their gaming screens. Too bad they might never taste that lemonade or those roast beef sandwiches.

I check my mirror for speeding convertibles and pull back out on the side road, headed back to the city. Strange, it feels like shafts of straw and chaff are prickling the sunburn on the back of my neck, it was a better daydream than I thought. At least that's what McGregor says.

Movies and Memories

Every once in a while you read a news item about an anniversary of an event or hear a radio announcer tell you it was so many years ago this song was released and you hear yourself saying. "That can't be right."

Even when investigation reveals the information is correct, we tend to scroll back through our memory banks and try to place the dates in perspective wondering where the years went and how they could have passed so quickly.

This recent news item told me that it in a few weeks it will be the 40th anniversary of the release of the movie American Graffiti. The movie came out in August 1973 and launched the career of Harrison Ford, Susanne Somers, Richard Dreyfuss and others.

But more important it took the baby boomer generation back to a night in 1962 and let us all relive of those magic summer nights when the most important things in life were gas in your tank or whether the right person would smile at you and say 'hi.'

I have the movie in VHS and DVD and I will watch parts of it or all of it when it's on as a movie of the week or filling in a late night program slot. Every time I watch it I am pleased to see or hear some little nuance that I have missed before.

Maybe something hanging from a car mirror or the design of a car club plate or jacket will bring a smile. Maybe it's a shot of a guy with his arm around his girl turning the corner with his other hand on the "necker knob" attached to his steering wheel, or the carhops on roller skates. The movie floods you with images from your past.

In two hours, the movie condenses one weekend evening and jams in all the teen-age trials and tribulations that we all went through. It brings back those nights when we fell in love at 9:00 PM and broke up just after midnight. It reminds us of the varied late night conversations that changed our life's plans two or three times during the evening.

A Fraser Valley car buff has recreated the yellow Ford coupe hot rod and the black 1955 Chevy that played out the final drag race on Paradise Road. His plan is to take the cars to California to the road where the race was filmed and recreate that early morning epic battle.

The scene had everything. It was evil against good, Ford against Chev, the bad guy stealing the good girl and the hero coming to the rescue. A Shakespeare play with hamburgers and rock and roll music.

Even though the movie is set in small town USA, it was small town everywhere. In Langley, our Paradise Road was a stretch of Latimer road between 36th and 40th. Avenues.

Summer Sunday afternoons the cars would stage in the open field and the races went on until the RCMP showed up.

It didn't matter what the name was on the hamburger joint in the movie. Every town had one or two. There were some serious discussions took place there but they didn't involve mortgage rates, childcare, health issues or deadlines. That's why we like to climb into that movie and escape back to those times.

The movies and the songs may be old but the memories are good ones. At least that's what McGregor says.

Finding That Perfect Spot

Sunday afternoon the sun popped through the clouds just after the Blue Jays lost. I had 2 hours before the Lions game and I had three chapters left to finish the book I was reading. I was close to finding out if she jumped or was pushed.

I took my book out to the deck but the neighbourhood was buzzing with a summer day's activities and I thought about finding a perfect spot to read. I remembered a quiet place I had seen on one of my walks through south Campbell Valley Park so I grabbed a lawn chair, a jug of ice tea and my book and headed south.

There were lots of cars in the lot but my spot was peaceful with only a slight murmur of the poplar leaves whispering to each other. I placed the chair so the angle of the sun through the trees fell across the pages of the book. I found my place and walked alongside the detective for a bit.

A young couple came around the corner carrying a blanket and a picnic basket. They seemed surprised to see me and carried on across the field. As they spread their blanket I thought of other the summer picnics. Some intimate and secluded like theirs, others boisterous, with multi generations consuming too much food, playing softball and talking 'til dark.

I started reading again and realized I had read that page and searched for where I had left off. The conversation of the trees was rudely interrupted by a Westjet aircraft flying low and slow on descent to Abbotsford. It seems this perfect spot is on their flight path. I watched it disappear and thought about friends I have returning from holidays and friends I have leaving. The breeze has flipped the pages and I again have to find where I was.

Then I heard a voice over a microphone from behind me telling the guests to be seated followed shortly by an organ playing the wedding march. Someone has chosen a beautiful day to be married in the park. My mind wanders to outdoor weddings I have attended in scorching heat and driving rain and I recall hearing that sun, or rain, on the bride is good luck.

The detective and I are heading down an alley when a Mom and Dad and two little girls walk by. The smallest falls down and says she is not walking anymore. Dad says he will leave her there but every kid in the world knows they won't ever be left behind. He picks her up and doesn't yet realize he will pick up his daughters every time they fall, no matter how old they are.

Suddenly there is loud conversation and laughter and a woman's voice says. "Right over here, the light is perfect this time of day." A photographer leads the wedding party into my spot for pictures. Guessing they don't want someone in shorts and sandals and t-shirt in the background, I smile, wish them good luck and pack up.

I have read a total of nine pages that I will have to read over. Not a great spot for reading but there seemed to be lots of memories falling from the branches that afternoon.

The great thing about fictional detectives is that you can walk away from them anytime and they won't do anything until you get back. At least that's what McGregor says.

Summertime Car Shows

On a late summer Friday night a group of us were relaxing in lawn chairs, sitting behind our old cars and trucks at a Tim Horton's. These weekly mini car shows pop up around the community during the summer months, all of them a build up to the Langley Good Times Cruise-in coming this weekend to downtown Langley.

It's been a great outdoor summer and we've all had lots of opportunity to show off our vehicles across the lower mainland and some have even gone farther afield as many cities across the province have added a car show to their summer schedule.

You might think that we would eventually run out of things to talk about but someone might show up with a different vehicle or maybe someone has just finished a project car and they are showing it off for the first time. Of course everyone seems to always be doing some sort of repair or restoration or looking for parts or advice. There is never a shortage of advice when car people gather.

No matter what you need done to your vehicle you will find the expert at one of these shows. There is the engine guy, the paint guy, the transmission guy or the upholstery guy. All you have to do is ask someone and you'll find the right guy.

I personally like the urban legend stories. Someone always seems to know where there is a secret cache of vehicles or maybe that one classic tucked away. "I know someone who knows where four of those trucks are but the husband and wife passed away and the estate is tied up in court so you can't get at them."

Or, "I know where you can find one of those cars. My friend knows a guy who lives by an old lady who has one in a garage but it belongs to her son who she hasn't seen in years so she won't sell it." Sometimes the stories are true sometimes they don't pan out, but searching them out is the fun part.

For instance, I have the wrong tailgate on my truck. The word Ford should be in script not block letters as it's from a newer model. Many folks go out of their way to point this out. I get lots of tips where I might find the right one.

I went to Yarrow and looked at one that was in worse shape than mine but the drive was nice. I went to Whonnock to a wrecking yard where it wasn't the right tailgate but I found some other stuff. I followed a tip to Hope and found one that was attached to a truck but he wanted to sell the whole vehicle only.

But it wasn't a wasted trip because they were a great couple and they had lots of old signs and memorabilia to walk through. I could simply buy a 'new old tailgate' but then what excuse would I have for taking off on a weekend exploration? Looking for a tailgate occupies a lot of afternoons throughout the dreary winter.

For all of you coming down to the Cruise in this weekend, I know I have the wrong tailgate on my truck, you don't have to point that out, but check out my 8-track under the dash, it works and sounds great.

Check out downtown, it's a trip back to a simpler time. At least that's what McGregor says.

Time to Slow Down and Take it Easy

When you become a senior, you have to keep on your toes, look for bargains, deals, discounts or perks. There are plenty of opportunities out there to save a dollar or maybe make your life a bit easier.

Last week, the Environment Police issued an Air Quality Advisory stating: 'Persons with chronic underlying medical conditions should postpone strenuous activities until the advisory is lifted. Staying indoors in air-conditioned spaces helps to reduce fine particulate exposure. Exposure is particularly a concern for infants, the elderly and those who have diabetes, and lung or heart disease.'

As a senior, I don't have to read the whole advisory but I can pick out the message that says: The elderly should postpone strenuous activities, staying indoors in air conditioned spaces, until the advisory is lifted. Pretty much sounds like a week off for me.

The lawn is looking a bit ragged, even though the grass is dying the dandelions and weeds are still growing strong.

But with that high particulate content in the air, should I risk trudging through the haze behind the mower? I think not.

Cooking is out of the question. No sense in raising the temperature in the kitchen and I can only imagine the damage to my lungs of inhaling BBQ smoke on top of the forest fire fumes. I might risk making my way out to my vehicle and heading out to an air-conditioned restaurant.

Staying inside is a great chance to catch up on reading, writing and watching old movies. You might even say that showering and shaving are strenuous activities so maybe forget that for a few days and just hang out in shorts, sandals and a t-shirt. The other patrons and staff in the restaurants will let you know when it is time to risk cleaning up a bit.

Life is never fair. When we get nice weather, it gets too hot then the smoke rolls in. If we find a nice beach, there is swimmer's itch or an e-coli warning posted. Summer holidays are never like the adventures in the travel magazines.

I recall zipping along the highway in our truck and camper making great time anticipating an early arrival at our campsite then rounding the corner and coming up behind a long line of vehicles all stopped for paving or blasting or some other road enhancement project heralded by the big sign, "Sorry for the Inconvenience, P.A. Gaglardi."

I doubt Mr. Gaglardi was ever stuck in a truck and camper in 90 degree heat with two hot, cranky little kids. Inconvenience is not even close to describing the experience.

In the old days, before the Coquihalla Highway, you came home on either the Fraser Canyon or the Hope-Princeton highway. Many a camper, returning from holidays, has spent a Sunday afternoon ten miles east of Hope in bumper to bumper traffic as both highways merged at the junction in Hope. Never a great way to end a perfect vacation.

Measuring the good with bad and making the best of the situation is what we call 'Life' and no one ever promised it would be fair all the time. Sometimes we just have to be reminded to slow down a bit.

That's enough writing for now, I'm feeling a bit faint and the jug of ice tea is calling my name. No sense overdoing it while the advisory is still in effect. At least that's what McGregor says.

Jim McGregor

Lazy Days of Summer
Were Always Busy

I ran across an article warning parents about the dangers of
children having "idle hands' during the summer. The
premise of the report tells us that today's children, with
their obsession with electronics, can become isolated during
the summer vacation period and spend too much time in
their rooms, connecting with friends electronically rather
than face to face.

I let my mind wander back to the summer vacations of
my youth and the most common phrase that kept coming
up was, "You kids get outside and find something to do or
I'll find something to do for you!"

I was reading a novel set in the fifties, and the Mother
yelled at her kids, "Wash your hands and feet and get up to
bed." I'd forgotten about black feet. Spending all day
without shoes and socks on, road tar, tree sap and good old
dirt would turn the soles of your feet black from June to
September.

A summer day would start with chores, usually in the garden. By August, beans were ready. Green beans, yellow beans, pole beans and picking the bush beans meant you also got your knees dirty. Once a couple of pans of beans were plucked from the vines, you had to tip and tail them and cut them up for canning or freezing.

This was all done in the early morning before the heat of the day and, while we were chopping beans on the covered back porch we would discuss the plans for the day.

Some days it was just a continuation of the game of scrub we had started the day before. Slowly everyone would gather, some brought balls, some bringing bats. Pieces of plywood or burlap sacks would serve as bases on the well-worn base baths and, without backstops or umpires, the game would resume.

Maybe it was day for bike riding. Bikes were amazing pieces of transportation and they weren't speciality pieces of equipment like BMX or mountain bikes or expensive road racing bikes. The bikes of my youth had fenders and the chain guards that were held on by a twisted piece of wire. The seat was wrapped in tape and the headlight never stayed pointing straight.

Those bikes could go anywhere. They could fly across ditches, race through the neighbour's fields, negotiate the trails through the blackberries and if you slammed on the brakes on a gravel rode you could spin them around, raising a cloud of dust.

We had secret forts in the bushes surround by bugs and wasps and spiders. We had dangerous forts in the trees with splinters and nails sticking up everywhere. We had gravel pits full of rust colored water and we had rivers with slippery banks and strong under currents.

I don't recall ever having to call for an ambulance or Search and Rescue to rescue me, or one of my friends. Even though we had all of those dangers around us we also had something called 'common sense.' If someone got hung up, we figured it out and the last thing we needed was our parents finding out.

If my hands were idle on a summer day, they were usually turning the pages of a book. Maybe that is why I don't like to sit and do nothing in my retired years. There is just too much to do out there.

Bring your glove and ball over; we can play 'til its dark. At least that's what McGregor says.

When the Sun Gets Too Hot

It's a silent, sunny, Sunday afternoon and as Paul Simon would say, "I have no deeds to do, no promises to keep." Looks like a chance to position my lounge chair out in the sun and catch some rays.

I pull on some shorts and lather sunscreen on my face, neck and shoulders and head for the deck. The smell of sunscreen on a hot day transports me back to Penticton on those endless summer days when we would leave Langley on a Friday afternoon. Days and nights would blend together. The girls would look like they had walked out of Coppertone ads and they smelled like coconut or some other exotic scent. We would drive home Sunday, tired, blistered and burned.

The afternoon sun is hot on my skin and I remember family picnics, shirtless and shoeless where the baseballs and footballs filled the air and we played hard all afternoon, oblivious to the baking our bodies were taking.

That's the freedom I want to relive today, just lying in the sun, oblivious to time, no responsibilities nowhere to be.

Reclaiming those convertible days when you spent the night in a sleeping bag in the back seat and if a girl asked you to put lotion on her back that was the highlight of your weekend. "Looking for fun and feeling groovy."

With my lounger reclined and my book and ice tea strategically located, I collapse back and close my eyes. The sun begins its magic and before long the knot fades from my shoulder and my wonky knees seem to be healing as I lie there. This is great.

It lasts for five minutes. I think the tops of my ears are burning and my lips feel like they are cracking. I open my eyes and go blind for a second it's so bright. Some kind of a bug is stuck in the sunscreen on my cheek and sweat is rolling down from my forehead and underarms. I pull my chair into the shade, re-position my drink and pick up my book. Maybe they're right, maybe it is hotter than it used to be.

Before I start reading, I see another vision of that Penticton beach. If I look past the bronze girls I see some older men in straw hats, shirts and shorts and socks and sandals sitting under umbrellas. If I take a second look at that family picnic and look past the flying Frisbees I see Aunts and Uncles and Grandmas and Grandpas sitting in lawn chairs in the shade of the fir trees. How come I never noticed them there before?

It's tough when your mind wants you to run across the hot sand and dive into the cool lake but reality is telling you to limp over and put your lawn chair in the shade.

As I start to read, I start to nod off and a long ago voice says "Quiet, let Grandpa have a nap." I refuse to be that

Grandpa and I open my eyes wide and take a long, cold drink. When I wake with the book on my chest, my cell phone says I slept for about twenty minutes.

Sometimes when you are in a garden centre you will see a sign beside a plant that says, "For best results, plant in a spot with equal sun and shade." I have to find that spot on my deck. At least that's what McGregor says.

Ice Cream on a Hot Day

It's always nice to wake up to sunshine on a day when you have an outdoor activity planned. Last week, vendors and organizers of the annual Art's Alive were most pleased to be able to set up and display on a gorgeous August day.

Natasha and I had fun selling our books, photography, poetry and talking to old friends and making new ones. Creative people are usually poor salesmen and a kind word about our display is often taken as payment as gratefully as cash. Hence the term "starving artists".

The sun brings out a great crowd and smell of food from ethnic venues and the sound of music from various sources adds to the festival atmosphere as people flit from booth to booth like bees in a flower garden, each one finding something, shiny, warm, or colourful to suit their fancy and take back home.

As the hot afternoon winds down I am returning to our display from a tour and I see an ice cream truck parked in the shade. I think I will buy a cold treat for Natasha and I and Ken in the next booth. As I approach the truck, I recall memories of standing at the end of the driveway, holding tightly to little hands as the kids watched the jingling truck approaching. There were always quarters and fifty cent pieces in the dish on the window sill, specifically saved for the ice cream man.

I recall one man saying that his Dad had told his five kids that when the Ice cream truck was playing music, it was telling people he was out of ice cream so there was no need to go running out there. Well played, Dad. He probably saved a big chunk of cash over the summer.

When I get to the truck, I see his display of popsicles, revels, fudgsicles, cones and ice cream sandwiches. I have always been partial to revels even though I often end up with a flake of chocolate on my shirt.

"Three revels, please," I ask and take a five dollar bill out of my wallet. The man opens his freezer and pulls out three revels, considerably smaller than I remember and says. "Twelve dollars please."

I look at the fiver in my hand and some options quickly form in my mind. Natasha and Ken don't know I'm buying them a revel so I don't really have to, I could just buy one, find some shade and finish before I got back to the table. I could protest loudly about the outrageous cost of Ice cream and walk away. Or, remembering that it's the thought that counts, I could just carry on as planned.

I take another ten from wallet, knowing I'm cutting deeply into my net profit for the day, and take the revels back where they are received with great fanfare and many thanks. I don't mention the cost or share my observation that I'm surprised ice cream is not sold from Brinks' armoured cars these days.

Packages are smaller, prices are higher and we old timers shake our heads thinking about the father of five kids standing at the end of the driveway today with twenty dollars in his hand.

But the one thing that will never change is the smile on someone's face when you give him or her an ice cream treat on a hot day, that's priceless. At least that's what McGregor says.

The Great Escape

I was at the gas pumps one day and while my hard earned cash was flowing into my fuel tank, I found myself admiring the motorcycle at the adjacent pump. Behind the seat there was a sleeping bag, a tent and a duffle bag attached to a rack with an intricate web of bungie cords and no doubt the saddlebags were full.

The owner came out and I noticed he had on some very serious leathers and Dayton boots. As he pulled on his gloves he nodded and I said, "Looks like you're leaving town." He smiled and said he was headed for Newfoundland.

It seems his job in the gas fields north of Fort St. John had dried up so he traded his 4x4 for this sport touring bike and came home to gather his things together before heading east.

He had no plan, no GPS. He had no reservations at campsites or motels. He had no estimated time of arrival or date of return. He was simply driving across Canada. He shared, "I'm watching for the breaks in the clouds and following the sunshine across the country." What an adventurous quote.

I wished him luck as he fastened his helmet and gave him a wave as he pulled out on to the highway. Driving home, I recalled those footloose and fancy-free days.

I remembered being 21 when my buddy Fred bought a brand new Plymouth Barracuda and we decided to drive it to Tijuana and back, just because we could. No route planning, no reservations just threw some clothes in the trunk, turned on the tunes and headed south.

Another time my buddy Mike and I went camping but didn't know where we were going. We ended up in Banff and then camped wherever on our way back. Lots of adventures on both trips but we all survived the accidents and incidents and getting lost but, most of all, finding our way.

My Dad used to read all the Louis L'Amour western novels and I never saw the connection until I read one myself. For a man with six kids who drove truck all day and came home to his farm, I could see the attraction of a lone character tying his horse to a tree branch, bedding down beside a campfire under the stars on the wide open prairies.

L'Amour's characters didn't have mortgages or utility bills or kids with dentist appointments and school expenses. I realized that Dad slipped into the pages of those books and mounted up beside the gunslingers or the Texas Rangers and rode off into the sunset.

At a recent car show there was a 1972 Econoline van for sale. It was what we used to call a "shaggin wagon". Fridge, stove, bed, low mileage, and low price. I looked at that thinking, "I'll bet I could get to Newfoundland and back in that with no problem."

Once in a while, you have to escape. At least that's what McGregor says.

FALL

The Seasons Go Round and Round

A dry stick snapped and the brambles shivered as a small animal scurried down the bank toward the creek. "Probably a rabbit" he thought. There used to be all sorts of animals sharing his bush, but now, not so many. How long had it been since he'd seen a pheasant?

Less bush and more houses had chased the deer and the coyotes deeper into last bit of forest that remained. Not like when he first bought the place. A fall morning like this would see herons beside his pond or deer at the edge of the trees nibbling his lawn.

He dumped the potato skins and orange peels from the plastic ice cream bucket into the compost. This was his big chore of the day now, the walk out to the compost. He set his cane against the fence wire and leaned back on the box. He would have to rest to catch his breath and gather strength to get back to the house.

He stretched his back and gazed up at the tops of the fir and spruce trees poking into the sky. Forty feet tall, they stood like guards at attention on either side of his property.

He could remember placing them in the ground as seedlings. Pounding in stakes to keep them straight and giving out endless warnings to rambunctious boys not to disturb them.

As he watched, one of the boys darted out of his memory for a long pass, another faded to the left to catch a long fly ball, both of them barely missing the young trees. The picture was so vivid he almost yelled at them to be careful.

They had always complained about the obstruction the seedlings presented. In their youth, they could not see the future he was seeing for the trees or the invisible stakes he had placed beside the boys to keep them growing straight.

As they disappeared into the mist, he realized that they were now as mature as the trees, protecting seedlings of their own. Yet, they still found time to stop by, not so much to visit any more, but to cut lawns, prune trees, exercise the weed eater and plant and water the garden. The jobs he used to do.

He turned to look at the garden, almost finished planting but that was a tedious job now. How many bags of vegetables had he loaded into the trunks of visitor's cars over the years?

He watched himself guide the rotor-tiller in straight black furrows in the spring. He remembered the days he would be walking out from the corn behind the wheelbarrow, arms straining with a load of pumpkins, marrows, squash and squealing grandkids just in time for Halloween.

Now, a plastic pail of table scraps was a full load.

He squeezed a gnarled hand around the cane and lifted himself up to a steady balance. As he headed back to the house he stopped to watch himself go by astride the riding mower in the summer sun. He could smell the sweat and the gas and the oil. He looked around and remembered how good it looked, mowed and trimmed, and the satisfaction of a job well done.

He continued back to the house. He knew she was watching from the kitchen window. She trusted his steel hips less than he did. If he went outside, she would find laundry to fold, dishes to dry or phone calls to make, chores that would let her watch from the window.

She never came right out and said they should sell, that would be his decision. She would once in a while mention that a call should be made to Carolyn, their realtor friend, just to get an idea of what it might be worth. He knew that call would start the snowball rolling down the hill.

As he reached the back of the garage he turned slowly and thought he could trace a smell of smoke to the fire pit. There the family gathered around on a late October days to clean up the branches and debris, roast wieners and talk until the embers of the fire died late in the evening.

The smoke cleared and he was amazed to see the sun was fully out and streaming down on the alders and cottonwood at the back of the property. They were alive and swaying effortlessly in the wind. The grass was suddenly greener and the gentle breeze wafted one memory after another across the scene.

An empty lot became a park like yard. A foundation soon supported a house, which became a loving home to a large extended family. The feeling of loss was slowly replaced with a huge sense of accomplishment and completion. He realized the seasons of his life were turning once more.

It was time to move on.

He wiped his eyes and nose with the ever-present hanky in his back pocket and headed up the ramp to the back door. Inside, he placed the cap and jacket on their respective hooks, set his cane in the corner and shuffled over to the coffee pot.

He poured a cup and quietly stirred in the milk. Looking out the window, as the season passed, with an almost indiscernible catch in his voice he said, "Well Mother, I guess you should give Carolyn a call today."

Back to School

He sat down next to his mother and was quiet for a minute.

"What's troubling you son?" she asked.

"I don't want to go back to school." He said firmly. "None of the kids like me."

She patted his hand. "I'm sure they do, it will be just fine.' She reassured.

"No Mom, the teachers don't like me, the bus drivers don't like me and even the custodian won't talk to me, I'm not going back to that school!"

His mother took a deep breath, turned to look at him and said quietly, "Son you have to go back to that school, that's your job, you are the Principal."

At this time of year we are busy shopping for school supplies, buying new blue jeans and running shoes, or listening to forecasts predicting nothing but sun for the next two weeks. We send our kids off to school assuming everyone there is ready and willing to receive them.

My sister taught for thirty-five years. Some insight from her includes the excitement of organization the week before, preparing a warm and welcome classroom. The mixed emotions of sharing their summer adventures while worrying about class sizes, or the student's acceptance of their new teacher. Would there be special needs kids and support for them, were her own kids having a good first day at their school, would new math or reading programs require extra prep time? Today's teachers, like her daughter, worry about funding cuts, strikes, personal safety and demanding parents. How will the new year go? She tells me that reassuring smiles from parents and students are always welcome on the first day.

My grandson is starting kindergarten next week. I asked him about this new adventure and he showed me the calendar with his first day marked on it. He told me he had scoped out the playground and knew who was going to be in his class. I asked him what he was going to learn, he shrugged and said, "I don't know, whatever they want to teach me I guess."

There it is. What an ominous responsibility yet amazing opportunity for his teachers. This is where their passion lies, to teach. Brand new students will be sitting in those desks like empty wide mouth Mason jars waiting to be filled. The teachers have this incredible orchard of ripe knowledge that they can pluck, peel and pack into those fragile waiting vessels. I'm sure there must be some frustration for teachers that these treasures cannot be preserved but, have to trust instead, that they will be opened with care at home.

In Robert Fulghum's book, *All I Really Need to Know, I Learned in Kindergarten,* he tells us that countries and corporations and families were given the answer to success by teachers years ago: 'Share everything, Play fair, Don't hit, Put things back where you found them, Clean up your own mess, Don't take things that aren't yours, Say you're sorry if you hurt someone, Wash your hands, Flush, Warm cookies and milk are good for you, Draw, paint, sing and dance, Take a nap, and, When you go out into the world, watch out for traffic, hold hands and stick together.' We learn this at the age of six, but it doesn't make sense until much later.

We buy the teachers a gift at the end of the year, maybe we should start thanking them for returning in the fall; at least that's what McGregor says.

Teaching the Kids

Those people you see smiling and humming are parents of children going back to school next week. I have a grandson starting Grade 1 and a son going into Grade 12; I can assure you that only one of them is excited about September's arrival.

We will give our children up to the teachers and expect the best. We will trust them to produce scholars and artists and musicians and send them back to us when they are finished. But don't we, as parents, have a bit of responsibility here too?

A few years back I was driving from Quesnel to Prince George on the way to my sister's retirement. She was completing thirty plus years as an elementary school teacher and I was thinking of something to say at her banquet. I had been at a four-day conference with best intentions of writing something but I just hadn't got around to it.

The car radio crackled off and on, picking up CBC radio here and there when suddenly it came in very clear and an announcer began a story about a man who was home with the flu, looking after his five-year-old son. The boy was glad to have dad home and was driving him crazy. The father picked up a kid's place mat from a restaurant on which the boy had colored a map of the world. He cut out the countries like a jig saw puzzle, set some scotch tape and the place mat pieces on the table and told the boy to put the puzzle together; this would surely give dad a break.

In about two minutes the boy came to dad, the puzzle was done and done perfectly.

"You did a great job," praised dad. "It was easy Daddy; there was a picture of a boy and girl on the other side. I just made sure the kids were put together right, and the world turned out OK!"

I pulled the car over to the shoulder of the Caribou highway on one of those quiet stretches where the fields on both sides reach for miles into the trees, and I let those words settle. Pretty nice words to share with someone who had made a life putting kids together right. I had my words for the banquet and some thoughts to think about.

For the next few months, our kids will be spending more waking time with their teachers than us. They will be taught how to listen, how to watch, how to learn and they will be watching and listening to everything around them. Not just at school, but conversations at home, TV, video games, and movies. It's all part of their education, and we as parents are all teachers.

We can question the education system from the Ministry down to the local school boards and teachers and we can challenge them all to produce for us and our kids, but if we are simply going to drop them off in the parking lot and not accept some responsibility for how or what they learn when they get home, then we are wasting an opportunity that our children have that is the envy of many countries.

It doesn't really matter if they are starting grade one, grade12 or first year university, let's help the teachers put these kids together right and maybe, just maybe, the world will turn out OK. That's what McGregor says.

The Rising Cost of Crayons

There was a bit of morning fog and the evening coffee on the deck was a tad chilly. I had a suspicion that August was trying to sneak past us and creep quietly into September before we noticed.

Then as I was leafing through the flyers I noticed an ad for "Back to School". I smiled at that knowing that those frustrating days were long behind me. I can see me as a kid trudging behind Mom and Dad as Mom read from the list and Dad complained about the cost of crayons, glue, paste, pencils, and paper. Then of course there were all the new clothes and multiply that times five kids.

Then I could see me as the Dad, following my wife as she read from the list and I complained about the cost of everything. "An electronic calculator!? How the hell are they going to learn to add, subtract, multiply and divide if we give them all a bloody calculator? I learned to do math with a pencil and paper. When they get a job, is their boss going to give them a bloody calculator!?"

Of course I complained about the cost of new shoes, jeans, dresses, backpacks and winter coats. I had to, I was a Dad and that is what I had been taught to do.

But then I took a second look at that Back to School flyer and realized the ads were not about pencils or crayons and there was no mention of shoes or jeans, they were all about the electronic gadgets and computer related products that would promise "an A+ School Year."

Instead of paste and glue there were advertising iPads, smartphones, ear buds, flash drives, tablets, software, laptop bags, printers, selfie sticks and even an ergonomic mouse. As I checked out the prices, I realized I had gotten off easy paying a mere $15.99 for the Canon LC-33 Electronic Calculator I was forced to buy thirty years ago. I know that is the model number because I still have it here on my desk in my office and it still works just fine.

A quick calculation of just the first page of the ad (using the trusty LC-33) comes to over a $1000.00. I'm not buying back to school stuff but I'm having an anxiety attack for those Dads that are.

A survey shows that Langley elementary school students these days are required to buy almost $100.00 of school supplies and that doesn't include the electronic gizmos and gadgets.

I can remember having a supply closet at the back of the room in elementary school and we could get stuff we needed from there during the year. But each year, school supply budgets are reduced and many teachers will pay over $500.00 a year out of their own pockets to provide for classroom materials. A Federal Tax Credit of $150.00 was introduced this year for teachers who are buying supplies to be used in the classroom. I'll bet their spouses, most of them Dads, are complaining about the costs.

I'm sure we all remember the excitement of that first day of school showing up with new clothes, sharp pencils and a bag full of school supplies. But it's not cheap now.

Maybe those of us that remember those special September days can check with the local schools and find out which families might need some help putting those memories together. At least that's what McGregor says.

Remembering the First Day of School

Walking across the yard on a recent hot afternoon, a "dust devil" swirled across the dry lawn and garden and stirred up some dust and twigs and tugged a couple of almost orange leaves from one of the trees. It was followed by a gust of cooler wind, carrying a twinge of fall as it scooted across the yard toward the neighbour's.

I know there is still plenty of hot dry weather to come but the mini tornado also stirred up some late summer memories from years gone by. It was about this time of year that two or three of us guys would pedal our bikes down to Langley Central School to see if the class lists had been posted on the door.

It was the practice back in those days to display the class lists, teachers, and classrooms so the kids would know where to go on the first day. You often had to push your way through the crowd of kids, and some parents, who had come to get a preview of who would be in your class and who your teacher would be.

Would you be in the class with that jerk again this year? Would that special 'she' or 'he' be in your class? Would you have the cranky teacher or the nice teacher? What if they were a new teacher and you didn't know anything about them?

Sometimes you would ride home buoyed by the news that you had the best teacher and other times you were dejected and it looked like a long year ahead because you had the old grump and 'that special person' was in another class.

The most damaging year to my development was the year we were returning to Grade 7. We would be the Big Kids and how great that would be. On the first day of school, all the students who had signed up for band were called to the gym. They had built a state of the art band room at Langley High School and all the students from all over the District that had signed up for band were being put into two Grade 7 classes that would attend Langley High.

In one day, we had gone from being the Big Kids to the little kids. Even my sister in Grade 12 refused to acknowledge my presence in 'her school.'

Posting the class lists is a thing of the past due to privacy laws and the fact that the teachers have only a vague idea of who will be where on the first day of school. The students are advised to report to the classrooms they were in last year and when the staff has an idea of numbers, the assignments to classes are made.

To me, it seems being organized a week ahead was better for everyone but that was then, this is now. The first day can be stressful or delightful; either way, you'll remember it for years. At least that's what McGregor says.

Hold On to Summer

I woke up and it was cold in the house. I plucked my housecoat from behind the bedroom door and put a pot of coffee on to brew. My bare feet were cold so I went and put on some socks. The coffee took a bit of the chill off and I had a longer, hotter shower than usual and dressed before breakfast. It was still cold.

I could easily have remedied the situation by going to the thermostat and clicking the switch to on and the furnace would have kicked in and warmed up the house. But it wasn't October 1st yet. My kids will attest that each fall they regularly heard me echoing my Father's words, "Put on a sweater, put on some heavier socks, it's too early to put the furnace on."

I'm pretty sure it was a financial thing with my Dad and a long sleeve shirt and sweater were cheaper than sending the electric company more money. In the earlier days, living in our old draughty farmhouses, you could just throw another piece of firewood into the kitchen stove and it was comfortable if you stayed close, but firewood was much cheaper than oil or electricity.

For me it's a bit different. As soon as I turn that switch to on, summer is over. That's a signal that I've given in to fall and conceded that there will be no more days of sunshine to warm my house or my body. I'm not ready to change seasons yet.

At the end of a busy Cruise-in weekend we sat at the swap meet in the sunshine. My buddy Chuck was the DJ with a great selection of fifties and sixties songs and, in the words of Wolfman Jack, he encouraged the large crowd to "sit back and relax while I spin some tracks from my stacks of wax!"

Many of the vendors or customers stopped by to tell him how great the music was and how much it added to the beautiful day. It truly was a beautiful day, blue cloudless sky, warm sunshine and just enough breeze to whisk the brown and yellow leaves across the lot mixed with voices of Johnny Rivers, Smokey Robinson and Brenda Lee.

Everyone there had the same feeling; they didn't want summer to end either. It was almost as if the crowd was banding together to grab the edge of that late summer Sunday afternoon and stretch it out into next week and maybe the week after that.

No doubt it wasn't just the car show crowd. I'm sure gardeners were harvesting, hoping for just a few more pleasant days before the cold rain. Probably, Campbell Valley Park and the Fort to Fort trail were busy with walkers and dogs and kayakers and paddlers were out on the channel and the lakes taking advantage of calm water and enjoying the breeze at their back and the sun on their neck.

There is almost a sense of desperation for those who promised themselves they would be out more this summer and have suddenly realized they didn't do near as much as they wanted to, and now they are chasing the shadows as they get longer and disappear earlier.

Dig out some heavier PJ's and spread another blanket on the bed. The long range forecast looks promising. Don't give in; hang on to summer as long as you can. At least that's what McGregor says.

200

The Intruder

Something happened to my trees last night! I remembered being apprehensive about feeling a cool breeze just as I was closing windows before bed, almost a foreboding. This morning, a mist hung over the back yard, a sheer curtain hiding the trees from view.

I wasn't really sure where the sun was, maybe there, between the two tall firs, maybe higher. It was there somewhere, just not quite hot enough to burn holes through the gloom. But by the time my second cup of coffee was gone I glanced out the window to find the sun had taken charge now and only wisps of fog skimmed the lawn.

I started to turn away and then, quickly glanced back at my trees! Someone had been in my yard overnight! They had been up in the oak and maple trees, loosened some of the leaves 'til they fell, curled some, painted or tinted others, and scattered them in among the green ones!

I walked out onto the deck to take a closer look.

The grass was wet It had been dry last night and no rain had fallen. Dew maybe? No footprints. A small shudder in the branches raised some goose bumps on my arms and tumbled down a few more leaves onto the lawn. They had been remarkably well painted. Each one showing the transition from green to brown or red to yellow covering all the different shades in between all on each leaf. I'm sure if I fanned out four or five like playing cards, they would resemble paint swatches in a hardware store.

The gate was secure, no ladder marks on the lawn. Who could have taken the time, in the dark, to perform such an amazing feat? I looked down at the garden. They had been there too. Two or three of the reddest apples had been knocked to the ground, they probably bumped them when they were dabbing the pale yellow on the exposed side of the pears. They had spent a lot of time on the pumpkins. The biggest ones, now suddenly visible among the vines, had been brushed almost totally orange. Some of the smaller ones sported only splotches of orange or a splash of yellow overspray here and there.

I was not unhappy with what had been done. Whoever it was had a marvellous sense of balance and blending. So far everything seemed to be in harmony and I had a feeling they were far from finished. There was just a concern that I somehow wasn't ready for this to happen, that I had not given permission that it was happening too fast. I was not in charge.

My theories were interrupted by the geese gaggling overhead. I'd seen some yesterday too, in a large V. They appeared anxious these last couple of days, flying with purpose rather than in big practice circles.

Going out for the paper, I tentatively opened the front door, not knowing if the intruder had been here too. The small maple was untouched. The roses were still red or white. They hadn't been here yet, but I was pretty sure I could smell their presence. Not an easy scent to describe, much like the mist, there one minute, gone the next. I picked up the paper. September 23rd. it said. The first day of fall it said. Hmmm, coincidence I wonder?!

The seasons seem to be getting closer together, at least, that's what McGregor says.

Jim McGregor

High and Dry

October is Power Smart month and our Premier tells us that if we unplug our cell phone chargers each day we will save enough energy to power all the arenas in the NHL for many years to come. Somehow, I don't think this conclusion was developed by electrical engineers. It sounds more like something that came out of a Deputy Minister's Friday afternoon martini club.

"Hey Bob, let's tell them if they unplug their chargers, they can save money on their Hydro bills," "No, let's say they can power their house for a month!" "Hey how about their local hockey arena?" "Better yet, hockey season is starting, how about all the rinks in the NHL!?" "Yes, that's it!" Insert sound of glasses tinkling in a toast here.

My cell phone charger is plugged in behind my dresser and I just don't see myself moving that two times a day so, I will be relying on the rest of you to keep the red goal lights flashing across North America.

But I have a better idea. Recently, on a bright, breezy day I was driving along 8ᵗʰ. Ave. and spied a clothesline in the back yard of a tidy little farm. The wind had the towels snapping playfully at the sheets and the socks were mischievously kicking at the underwear.

If the Government passed a law that we could not use our dryers between June and October, but only use clothes lines, I'm sure we could save enough surplus energy to sale to the United States so that we would never have to pay a Hydro bill again! But, I'll double-check that with a couple of Deputy Ministers.

My Mom never had a dryer until she recently moved into her townhouse. With six kids and two adults, our clothesline was full all year round. My Dad knew that dryers required 220 volts and 220 was twice times 110 so he was convinced they would use twice as much electricity. He was often opinionated and had a stubborn streak, traits that I'm glad were never passed on to any of his children.

Clothes dried on a clothesline bring magic into the house. Pillowcases are full of smells and sounds that make for great dreams. Slipping under summer sheets feels like you are being covered with feathers at the end of a hot day. When you step out of a shower and bury your face in a sun drenched towel, you feel twice as clean and fresh, and pajamas, I'll give you a second to remember the comfort of pajamas fresh off the clothesline!

Recently, I've learned that you can buy clothesline kits with washstands and pulleys and line from local building supply stores, you can even match colors with your siding etc. I'm sure Ikea has Skor-Lund designer clothes pegs for the upscale yards and no doubt, someone would start a

205

company called Nature Dry Installations to come and assemble it all for you.

The only down side is the possibility of ignorant scrap thieves mistaking your clothes line for hydro or telephone wires and trying to steal them for salvage. However any of us who have ever put a ladder against a clothesline pole to untwist the wire and put it back on the pulley, knows how dangerous this can be.

Global warming? The answer my friend is blowin' in the wind! At least, that's what McGregor says.

In Control

It was a dark and stormy night; a wet, dark, chilly November Saturday night to be exact. How did it come to be November so quickly? I recall seeing a calendar recently that warned: "Caution, dates on the calendar are closer than they appear!" But I am in for the night.

I have on my warm socks and sweat shirt, my faded jeans and the couch cushions have been arranged just right. I reach over gently and with, a tender hand I caress the warm, smooth contours of the remote control and draw it close to me. Truly there is no greater invention in the last fifty tears than the TV remote control. This night, at 7PM the Canucks are on Hockey Night in Canada and the Lions are on TSN, simultaneously. This is the exact situation the 'previous channel' button was developed for.

Like a time traveler, I hear the last strains of the Star Spangled Banner from a rink in Colorado and instantly I am transported to BC Place as Oh Canada ends in a raucous pre-kick-off cheer. The only muscles moving in my body are attached to the tendons that allow the flexion of the index finger as it dances Liberace like across the keyboard of my remote. I celebrate Geroy's first touchdown and then take my seat in Denver just as Sedin scores his first goal of the night.

Network timeouts are two minutes long; injury timeouts can be longer. These are crucial as it allows time to refill beverage glasses or salsa dishes. However, with proper maintenance and logistics planning, fresh batteries and arrangement of furniture and clear cutting of plant foliage, you can operate a good remote through a clear sight line from the kitchen.

Earlier in the year, there was hockey, Sunday night football and a World Series game on at the same time. That trilogy taxes even the best channel surfer and demands an almost complete silence in the room to allow for maximum concentration.

Now, a football game has four quarters and a hockey game has three periods so the breaks in the action can be tricky to coordinate. But due to timeouts, injuries and coach's challenges on the football field, and fights and penalties at the arena, the half time and second period breaks are going to occur within seconds of each other, as rare as an eclipse.

As the gun and the siren sound, the coffee pot is filled and turned on, the Tupperware container is emptied onto the dish and slid into the microwave. Then a quick trip to the bathroom, next, downstairs to put the truck in the garage, lock things up for the night, make two quick phone calls, take the plate of food and the coffee cup back into the living room and I'm there just as the puck drops. A guy has to stay in shape for this type of adrenaline burst.

The night ends well as I see the Geroy's second touchdown and another Sedin goal. Both a Colorado forward and the Calgary kicker hit goalposts and the home teams win both games. I make one more trip to the kitchen to get a small ice pack to apply to the throbbing digit, hoping that the knuckle swelling will not affect the rest of the season.

The TV remote inventor should have won the Nobel Prize for Science. At least, that's what McGregor says.

Twilight

My fir tall trees have become very adept at gathering up the hot afternoon rays and filtering them up through their branches. This makes for cool, back yard evenings, perfect for reading or writing. This night as I am reading, I absently reach down to scratch my dog's ears as she lies down beside my chair, except, she isn't really there.

Three months ago, after sixteen years of being a friend, a confidant and a member of the family, her pain became too much for both of us to bear, and she was gone. But I am glad that Skeena has visited in spirit tonight and dropped this muse at my feet.

I now counsel people buying pets to let them into their homes but not their hearts. It is easy to put a dog outside of your house, but once they are under your skin, you are in big trouble. Our vet had a sign in his office: If you are running late and don't have time to say your normal daily prayer, just say, "Dear God, please make me the person my dog thinks I am!" That pretty much sums it up.

It's nice when friends, lovers, or family members that have left us, make those unexpected visits. Whether they slip in the back yard in the twilight of day, dance out of the car radio on a forgotten melody, or tap us on the shoulder with a scent of their perfume or after shave in a crowded mall, we always take that minute to smile and share a memory with them. I like to think of those visits as invitations, an offer for us to unburden ourselves with something that has been troubling us, or an opportunity to say those things we wish we had.

In the novel, 'The Fiery Cross' Jamie Fraser says to wife Claire, "When the day shall come, that we do part, if my last words are not, 'I love you,' ye'll ken it because I did'na have time." When we get those visits, I believe we are being given just a little more time.

For all of you who from time to time have visits from those who have left us, I have shared some of the words that tumbled from my trees that night. It is the quiet time when we have the visitors, they are never far away, at least that's what McGregor says.

Skeena

Go on ahead girl, no need to look back,
You know this path very well;
Just go over the bridge, you'll see up ahead,
There's a clearing at the end of the trail.

It's quiet in there, the sunshine is warm,
Gone is the cold and the rain;
You can pin back your ears, run with the wind,
Gone are the fences and pain.

I won't follow today, but now and then, listen,
The sound of my footsteps will tell,
When I'm crossing the bridge, coming to meet you,
In the clearing, at the end of the trail.

Be Prepared

Some of us were without power for a while after the first nasty storm of the winter. Our neighbourhood was blacked out for twenty-four hours, some people less and some not at all. Storms are funny that way.

Disasters pay no heed to provincial borders, city limits or the price of the homes in your particular area. The wind could care less whether you have a new baby in the house and flood waters aren't the least bit interested if you are an old lady living alone or a farmer with a prize dairy herd. Fire destroys heirlooms with the same disdain that it consumes garbage, and earthquakes pay no heed to what is above them.

In my days of working with Emergency Planning, I would often have to speak to groups about preparedness. They were difficult sessions to organize because people don't usually line up to hear Emergency Planners speak. Most of the audience would resemble Chicken Little's farmyard friends, checking their watches and wondering how big the acorn was that landed on this guy's head.

Disasters don't happen to us. If the storm winds are going to be 90K, that will be somewhere on the island or up the valley. If the 'Big One' is going to shake the daylights out of us in the next fifty years, well, that is fifty years from now isn't? If the river is ever going to peak above the dyke level, it might do so next year, but not today.

Most Canadian cities budget more for garbage pick-up and animal control than they do for emergency planning. Most Canadian businesses budget nothing for business resumption plans. I have watched many small business owners stand in disbelief as the fire in the store next door has shut them down indefinitely. When your computers are melted to the desks, it's too late to think about backing up files or where you can go so your customers can find you.

The Value Village organization was an exception. While their building was still burning, obviously to be destroyed, their human resources staff had secured a meeting room, called in all the staff and told them what the plan of action was for the next day. They didn't want to lose their most important assets, their people, or their customers.

Do you have an alternative heating or cooking source or extra canned goods and water for seventy-two hours? Do you know how to open your garage door manually? If the cash and debit machines are down, for three days, what will you do? What about your insulin or your heart pills? Got enough baby formula or a good first aid kit? Ask yourself these questions now, while the sun is shining. Your Emergency Planning office has the answers.

Seventy-two hours is the time it may take emergency first responders to get to your door. You are expected to be able to be on your own for that period of time. If you're not prepared to do so, you become part of the problem pretty quick. We are too accustomed to picking up the phone and expecting the five-minute response because surely, the storm is going to hit 'somewhere else.'

We are told to expect more rain, more falling trees, and more power outages. Yep, it looks like the sky is falling, so get your ducks in a row.

If we fail to plan, we plan to fail. At least, that's what McGregor says.

Jim McGregor

Apples

I committed a sin as old as the Bible the other day; I stole an apple from a tree. Well, I really didn't steal it, the branch was hanging across the fence and I only had to step across a small ditch so I guess I really wasn't trespassing. But that's human nature isn't it? We massage our sins and rationalize and justify them until they are just indiscretions.

As I was leaning on the fence post munching on my prize, I surveyed the sad sight in front of me. The tired house was boarded up and the weathered barn was wide open. Where there used to be a lawn and garden were now waist high weeds and overgrown rosebushes. A pear tree drooped under the weight of scabby pears and the bees and wasps staggered drunkenly among the fermenting plums, which lie wasted on the ground. A rope with no swing hung from a maple limb and the whole scene was quiet. I knew it wouldn't be long until the development sign went up and the farm came down.

So much produce goes to waste in spite of the efforts of some who try to organize crop sharing or u-pick efforts.

Farmers now bring in pickers from other countries to pick our fruit so it can be transported to warehouses, shined and packed for the stores where we complain about the ridiculous prices.

I found myself remembering the fall clean up at Dad's place when we would crawl though the fence, trample the brambles and pick the apples growing on an old orchard tree. I have no idea what type they were but when you bit into them your lips pursed and your teeth tingled. We would bring a pail of these and a bucket of blackberries to Mom and she would do magic things with pastry.

I could only imagine the smells that used to come from the kitchen of this broken house, the pies in the oven, the shelves filled with jars of pears and plums.

I stepped up on the bottom fence rail and plucked one more apple for the road. When you have to work for it, rip your pant leg, scratch your arms and climb a branch or two, it just seems to taste a lot better. That's what McGregor says.

Jim McGregor

Jungle Apples

Across a field of long grass
Full of thistles and spiders,
Stands a weathered, old gnarled apple tree;
He scrambles up on Dad's shoulders
Shouts out, "Let's go!"
From there a jungle is all he can see!

Climb the rusted barbed wire,
Find the old orchard tracks,
Pull back the curtains of thick Ivy vine,
"There's a lot here for Grandma!"
He shouts out with joy,
"These big jungle apples look fine!"

Tangled, twisted old limbs
Hang heavy with fruit,
Enough to fill baskets and pails;
Then covered with grass stains,
Mixed in blackberry juice,
"We've got them all!" the little guy yells.

Then Grandma puts them in jars
Or spicy, hot pies,
So on Thanksgiving Day we will see,
What became of the treasure
He collected with Dad,
On his trek to the old Jungle tree!

Trees

The first blustery November morning blew in and I was drinking coffee looking out my kitchen window when a 50-foot fir tree toppled in my back yard. I had noticed this summer it was not in good shape and had contemplated taking it down. Now, Nature's Pruning and Falling Co. had done it for me, no charge. The only damage was to the weathered and faded plastic table and lawn chairs, which took a direct hit.

Immediately I was concerned, for this is Langley, on the west coast of Canada, and a tree had just come down! How long before protesters assembled in my front yard and petitions came through my mail slot? Here in B.C. it is assumed that that there is at least one spotted owl in each tree, at least one spawning salmon in each creek and it has been said you can't swing a cat without hitting an animal rights activist.

Don't get me wrong, I support environmental issues, I am concerned for our future; I just sometimes get confused on what issues I should support. For Instance "the friends of the park" are upset that trees have been cut. Yet a few years back when a baseball diamond and soccer field were removed from there, "friends of the park" protested that kids would have no place to play sports, trees and flowers would cost too much to plant and maintain, no road should go through the park and it should be left alone. Then the trees bloomed and the flowers blossomed and everything was OK.

Downtown, street trees were planted and declared beautiful in the fall, amazing when they were covered with Christmas lights, provided shady spots to sit in the summer, but then they grew. Did nobody see that coming? Now, they block the signs and the leaves make a mess on the sidewalks. Merchants want them taken out or cut back. Except of course for the merchants that don't have them in front of their stores, they want trees to put lights on. I see a need for huge pots with wheels and trailer hitches so trees can be dragged around from place to place, season to season.

Elsewhere in Langley, trees are cleared for houses. Areas are stripped and paved to build homes for the Hill People which means the Valley People get flooded when the heavy rains come and the water runs across land it in can no longer soak into. Attempts have been made to develop bylaws to regulate tree cutting but such regulations are not well received. The reason is because it is our neighbour's trees that are the problem. The neighbour's trees are dangerous, view blocking, sun screening hazards. We want to regulate their trees, not ours. Leave my yard alone please.

So it seems that the problem with trees is that they are in the wrong places. When someone wants to cut trees to *spruce* up a park and they go out on a *limb,* they are not very *poplar* and it won't be long until the *fir* flies.

Take charge, appoint yourself the *Branch Manager* of your yard and don't *bough* down to anyone. At Least that's what McGregor says.

Jim McGregor

Chan§in§ the Time

I was looking through a file of digital photos and came across a picture I took last January of my son shovelling snow in the driveway. I think I took the picture the picture for two reasons, number one, my teenage son was outside with a shovel in his hands and secondly, the snow piles along the driveway were about three feet high. Both of these scenes are very rare.

I had forgotten about those bleak, endless winter snow days. It's almost as if the continuous sunny days of summer had used their ultraviolet rays to fade those images from our minds. I have been ignoring the sideways rain, the wind and the wet leaves, pretending if I ignore them they will go away.

But this weekend is already Halloween. Then November is here whether we asked for it or not and whether we're ready for it or not. This weekend is also the time to turn our clocks from Fahrenheit to Celsius or whatever the heck we do with them at this time of year. I think it is 'Spring ahead, Fall back,' so I think we turn them back an hour, but I have never seen why we bother.

When the idea was first hatched back in the late 1800s the idea was to increase the daylight hours. Apparently some Australian entomologist convinced a whole whack of people that he needed more hours to catch bugs and that it would save on electricity by reducing the use of incandescent lights. The retail people, the recreational people, the trades people thought it was a great idea. Farmers weren't s pleased as the change upset milking and feeding times and I guess no one ever did get that old rooster to crow an hour earlier.

I wonder how people who emigrate here from non-Daylight Saving Time countries are affected. For instance, those 76 guys from Tamil that just arrived probably are just settling into a routine of showers, breakfast, exercise and rest periods and, wham, we upset their whole routine by turning the clocks back! No doubt an immigration lawyer will be all over Corrections Canada about this personal and emotional upheaval we have perpetrated on them.

Speaking of those Sri Lankan arrivals, what happened to the mechanics on board, the guys that kept that leaky rusted old freighter running all the way from Africa? Shouldn't they be forced to work for BC Ferries? Surely those guys have the mechanical ability to keep the fleet running from here to the Island.

Where was I? Oh yeah, the time change. We are not in for a good winter. Bad weather is again predicted, H1N1 is going to decimate our school and workplace attendances, the Olympics are going to bottleneck and strangle our traffic.

So here's what we do. We do nothing. We don't change our clocks in any direction. If it snows we stay home. If someone at work beside us sneezes, we stay home; if the traffic is stalled, we can longer phone from the car so we just go home. Once the Olympics start, we stay home and watch them on TV. It will work out fine if we all do it but if a few goody-two-shoes fight their way into work, it will spoil for all of us.

Don't change your clock this weekend; take the battery out altogether. We'll start again next April. At least that's what McGregor says.

Craft Sales

I don't know about you, but for me, once we get past the middle of November the days start to speed up. November slips into December and the next thing you know, it's Christmas Eve and time for me to start my Christmas shopping. Right about now, the Christmas craft sales and bake sales are ramping up and halls and gyms and lobbies become instant bakeries and department stores.

I have set up our book and art displays at a few of those in the past and we have sold some original Christmas cards and a few books. Our most popular book I refer to as our 'million seller' because we've sold a few but still have 'a million in my cellar.' If by chance you have ever had a booth beside me at a craft fair, you have probably heard that a hundred times.

I am a poor salesman. I tend to talk too much and not close the deal. A marketing consultant we talked to suggested that if someone picks up an item at your table, you have made the sale and must aggressively make sure the purchase is invoiced and bagged first, then start with the chit chat.

But that is not the atmosphere at most Christmas craft sales. Vendors are proudly displaying, pies and cakes, gingerbread men, knitting, handmade jewelry or art and they accept compliments and praise as grateful as they do cash.

Recently, the health inspector was in our church kitchen and suggested the ladies post a guideline for the allowable amount of trans fats that can be in items they were providing at luncheons or selling at bake sales.

Now, I respect the job of the inspectors, after all I was one for many years and many business owners were left scratching their heads at some of the regulations I tried to enforce. But, the next time you are at a bake sale, I dare you to ask the silver haired lady in the country apron what the trans-fat content is in that ten inch deep dish apple pie with the cinnamon and sugar glazed on the top.

I think if you look through the well-worn recipe books in your Mom or Grandma's kitchens, you'll find a lot of measures scattered throughout those tattered pages but probably not one table that calculates the trans-fat content of Christmas cake or lemon meringue pie.

Think how lonely you would be a table selling 'low fat Christmas pudding' or 'light Nanaimo bars.' Do you think anyone would buy your 'low calorie Black Forest cake?'

The attraction of the Christmas craft sale is that you can convince yourself you are going in there to buy gifts for other people when in reality, no one has any intention of making that baking last until Christmas. But once it's in the house, what the heck, it's still five weeks until Christmas and there will be plenty more bake sales.

We are in the downward spiral toward Christmas Day. The concerts, the parties the employee lunches all start coming at you pretty fast and they are laced with mince tarts, shortbread, eggnog and all with absolutely no regard to any trans-fat content.

The first things you should buy are a one size larger pair of slacks and a new belt. Go to a bake sale, buy a pie and get the season underway. At least that's what McGregor says.

Birds and Bees

I was digging some potatoes the other day when I noticed a large ripe pear lying on the ground. This was not too surprising as it was directly under a pear tree but what was interesting was that there hasn't been a pear on that tree for about four years.

One pear is not enough for pie or jam, so the most logical thing to do was peel it with my pocketknife and bite into it. The juice ran down my chin, I wiped it off with the back of my hand and gave thanks for such a delightful gift on a beautiful fall day.

The experts tell us that the reduction in fruit production is related to the declining bee population and due to "colony collapse disorder." I'm sure that term could be applied to many human households as well, a good description of day-to-day life for many families.

It seems mites, viruses, pesticides and poor nutrition cause this disorder that leads to less bees due to loss of habitat. I have another theory. I believe that the bee population is experiencing the X and Y generations of bees and these adolescent insects just won't get off their stingers and get to work. They are content to let the older generations leave early and work late resulting in elder bees that should have retired long ago, trying to keep up with the pollination demands.

Meanwhile, if the younger ones do leave the hive during the day, they find a clover bar and sit around knocking back nectar. The experts tell us that the females are the primary pollinators and most of the male's foraging is solely for his nourishment. Sound familiar?

A fellow in Victoria has invented a 'bee box,' a wooden hive designed with slotted trays that can be removed and cleaned of mites that will enhance the bee's survival rate. Great! Give these slackers a fine mahogany condo to lounge in and see how much work we get out of them then.

I think we have to shake up some hives, cut off the honey and get these guys back to work. At least, that's what McGregor says.

Jim McGregor

Lazzzzy!

I wonder if the bumble bee
Would just like to sit around?
Pull up a cloverleaf recliner,
On a quiet spot of ground.

There he'd sip a shot of nectar
Through a dandelion straw,
Relaxing, with his legs crossed,
There's a picture you could draw!

Rub some sunscreen on his thorax
Grab some grass and trim the blades,
Cut out some tiny, transparent lenses
For some funky, fescue shades!

He'd just ignore the pollination,
Forget his honey in the hive,
They'll think he's in the garden,
Won't expect him back 'til five!

But like me, just as he's dozing,
In this peaceful pastoral scene,
He's off his chair, back in the air,

The Kitchen Stove

A few summer days hung around and then left quickly. Overnight, the temperature dropped, the leaves fell, the rain came down and the protests started. The first complaints came from downstairs with my son urging me to turn the furnace on as his room was cold. Simultaneously, my old cat was sitting on the floor vents whining that no warm air was coming up to sooth his arthritic hip joints.

In response to all this I could hear my father's words coming from my mouth, "Throw another blanket on, put on a sweater, get up and do something." It wasn't October yet.

We are truly spoiled. We push a thermostat button to raise or lower the temperature or we flick a switch and on comes the gas fireplace to create a warm, comfortable ambiance and as long as the power doesn't go out we are happy.

I have had the pleasure recently to interview some seniors for a book project sponsored by Meals on Wheels, 'Reminiscing, Recipes and Remedies.' When the conversations come around to preparing food, the kitchen stove figures prominently in every story from every region.

Whether it was fuelled by dumping damp pails of sawdust into the hopper or by one of the children filling the wood box daily, the kitchen stove both heated the home and cooked the meals. It was on day and night, always with a big pot or kettle near the boil providing hot water for cooking, washing, or filling the Saturday night tub.

Because of the stove, the kitchen was the gathering place. Not just for family meals, the kitchen table was the place for homework, card games, visiting neighbours and often family counselling sessions.

If you woke in your upstairs bedroom to frost on the inside of the window pain and snow that had sifted in to powder the window sill, you knew it would be toasty warm down in the kitchen with a sizzling cast iron frying pan or pot of porridge ready to warm you from the inside out.

I recall wood trucks or sawdust trucks coming to our house. Companies like Garvin Ice and Fuel or Morrow Ice and Fuel, with the catchy slogan, 'Call to Morrow for your Ice Today;' they delivered to homes all over the lower mainland.

There were no buttons to push that split the wood and no switches to flick that shovelled sawdust into pails and the ice was carried to the sheds or ice boxes. One gentleman shared a summer memory of following the ice truck on their bikes. Every time the driver chopped off a block to be delivered, the kids picked up the scattered chips of ice and sucked them like candy or ice cream.

About this time of year the trunk with the woollen socks, the mittens and the long johns would make an appearance.

The woodshed would be full and the chimney would be cleaned. It wouldn't matter if the power went out, it would be warm in the kitchen.

I have the new furnace filter and the furnace will click on this weekend. In the meantime, I could send my son out to split wood and encourage the cat to go after the mole in my back lawn. Both of these activities would make them warmer and I'm sure the complaining would stop.

Until then, one more blanket and a sweater will do. At least that's what McGregor says.

Jim McGregor

Fall days and Festivals

A sunny October day seems to have a unique energy. It pulls you from your chair and tugs you outside, all the time reminding you that this may be the last nice day to plant bulbs, clean eavestroughs, or complete the yard clean-up. There is just enough crisp, liveliness in the air to make you consider a walk or a bike ride.

Even the couch potato sports enthusiast will stand on his deck with a coffee and struggle with the choice of the World Outside or the World Series. He will hear the warning in the branches of the nasty days to come and understands that his procrastinating ends this weekend.

Tens of thousands of people listened to the autumn message and headed for Fort Langley last weekend. Fort Langley is a pleasant destination any time of the year but, add eighty vendors, a food court, lively music and couple of tons of cranberries for sale, and you have a festival. The sixteenth annual Cranberry Festival to be exact.

I involve my friends in the activities I take on so when they need help they call in their favours. Unfortunately, my duties for this event did not include stages or microphones or tuxedos. At 5:00 AM I am headed to the Fort in work boots and blue jeans to install barricades, place generators, set up tables and chairs and show vendors to their locations.

It is dark and chilly and as I come across the Salmon River flats, a heavy mist is drifting into the town. I know from experience that this fall day could go in any direction in a few hours. The time goes by quickly and the move in goes smoothly. Then at 10:00 A.M, on cue, the sun burns through the fog and the festival-goers are treated to a splendid display of produce, crafts, smells, and music.

Before long the streets are choked, the booths are crowded and the shops and restaurants along the street are busy. There are lines ups for pancakes and cranberry sales and a crowd has gathered around the stage. Some folks trudge along complaining about how far away they had to park. They are passed by others striding along, faces turned to the sky and enjoying their morning stroll.

As I circulate through the crowd trying to avoid the taskmaster I am working for, I see bags being filled with preserves and jams and honey and vegetables. I hear recipes being traded and watch old friends renewing acquaintances. The little village is full to overflowing and it sparkles proudly against a backdrop of golden trees shining along the channel.

It is a family day and children ride the miniature train, play with the games or marvel at the 960 lb. pumpkin on display. I watch a four year old Asian boy clapping hands and tapping time while a champion fiddle player plays a catchy rendition of Five Foot Two, Eyes of Blue; a modern little boy enjoying a song from the 1920s.

As we leave the Fort at 7:00 PM, the tents are gone the streets are quiet; the music has faded up into the branches and the rain has started. But the exceptional fall day was not wasted and the sore muscles are just the sign of a job well done.

I hope you got everything done this weekend; after all you were warned. At least that's what McGregor says.

Pumpkin Faces

We were discussing pumpkins the other day, not an unusual topic for this time of year. I had no garden this year and the annual tradition of the grandkids, nieces and nephews coming for a wiener roast and getting their jack o' lanterns was approaching. Having just watched an episode of Bonanza where a bad guy "salted" a gold mine with his shotgun, making it look like there was real gold there, I knew what I had to do.

I zipped up to the pumpkin patch on a spectacular afternoon and picked out six pumpkins of equal size and a bunch of vines. Back home, I placed them strategically around in my bare garden plot and once again, the kids would have pumpkins.

While telling this story one of the listeners told us about her pumpkin that she was so proud of. I suspect there was a bit of disturbing attachment to her orange friend as she said she could not bring herself to cut it so she would just draw the face on. Then she said, "It has a bit of a rotten spot but I'll just hide that at the back so no one can see it."

But don't we all do that; paint on a presentable face and hide our rotten spots out of sight? Sure, some people have a happy grin carved on permanently and have absolutely no rotten spots at all. We like to be around those folks. They welcome us to their door, lighten our load and cheer us up.

Others have taken a jagged blade and gouged out a scowl that never seems to leave. We see them coming and we tend to look the other way, let someone else handle them. We hope they don't come to our counter or across our door. They leave a trail of garbage behind for us to clean up and their scowl starts to twist down the corners of our mouths as well.

Just like carving Jack O' lanterns we can choose the face we put on each day when we first look in the mirror. What should we be today? Maybe cranky and sour and starting to rot before we even leave the house or should we stretch that smile from ear to ear and open our eyes as wide as we can?

Most important is to not let someone else determine our face for us. Don't let anyone else's attitude influence whether you carve on a smile or a frown, you are the only one who can set your attitude for the day.

Most years, reading the pumpkins and peeking behind the masks ends on October 31st. But once every three years the faces keep coming at us right up until municipal Election Day.

I always give my best to all of the candidates and congratulate them on getting involved and making a difference. But I am always curious about those faces I see on the signs and in the ads. Are their smiles carved in or just painted on? Will they wash off and leave a scowl behind?

We all have to listen carefully and look closely at those that want to spend our money. Take a look through the eyes and see how bright the flame is inside and then, just to be sure, take a close look behind. There just might be a rotten spot hiding back there. At Least that's what McGregor says.

Slow Down, You Move Too Fast

I held the truck door as I closed it, and pushed it shut with a soft click. The silence was truly amazing and the slamming of a door would have been a rude intrusion. There were only nine or ten sites in the small campground, and yet here at three in the afternoon on a late September Thursday, I was the only one there.

The three-day seminar had been a disappointment so I had skipped out early and was attempting, once again, to make the Okanogan/Fraser Valley run in four hours. I had been doing well until Manning Park when I caught up to two Airstreams and a low bed. Impatiently, I took my place in line and said good-bye to the record attempt.

Now it was time for a pit stop and a stretch, let them get ahead and out of the way. I had passed this small campground dozens of times going and coming, but had never turned in. Today, it was in the right place at the right time.

I stretched and rubbed the knot above the left shoulder blade and took a look around. Beautiful tall trees were letting a few horizontal afternoon slivers of sunlight sneak through in scatters around the site.

Other than the distant sporadic traffic noise, the only other sound was a creek up ahead. A well-traveled path looked promising and I followed it to edge of the campsite in front of me.

The river's voice increased as I approached the edge. As I looked down about twenty feet, I saw the water sparkling and gurgling, over and around the rocks. Once again I felt like an intruder about to interrupt a casual conversation these old friends were having.

I made my way down the gravel bank. Some strategically placed smooth, flat stones provided a bridge to a large boulder in the middle of the river. I crossed to it knowing that right about now I would be yelling at my kids to be careful and stay off it.

Once on top, the view was most easily described as an autumn calendar page. At the coast, summer was hanging on like the last girl at the dance. Teasing, flirting, and promising to stay awhile. Here, higher and farther inland, the season changers had been hard at work for a couple of weeks. Painting, shading, redecorating for fall, and laying down a thick new carpet of needles and leaves. It was cool. Not chilly, not cold but refreshing after the stuffy air conditioning in the truck.

I had no camera and, worst of all, no fishing rod! The river ran helter-skelter up stream but as it approached the rock it became more serious and brought its arms together just in time to tumble over a small fall into a large pool. I found myself thinking that I was only an hour from home and I could probably back up early Sunday morning with the rod and the camera. Subconsciously, I knew that once I got back home, I would *"be too busy!"*

But if I did come back: *I would use worms or just a single egg, with a float and no weight. I would cast up stream into the current and let the stream carry the hook over the falls into the pool. The eddies would scoot it over to the dark emerald water under the log. The float would dive and the line would tighten! About the middle of the pool the trout would spiral out of the water and I would play it to me.*

As I removed the barbless hook I would marvel at its prism painted silver sides then cradle it back into the water, and with a flick and flash it would be gone. No such thing as a bad day fishing.

I think I felt the eyes before I actually saw them. A lone wolf stood on a log about 100 feet away on the other side of the river, watching me, probably smiling at my fishing story. He was mature and healthy and ready for winter. I wasn't even aware that there may be wolves in the area but there he was.

I strained into the surrounding bush to see if there were others, like the paintings in the malls. But somehow, I knew he was alone like me, the two of us just taking some time away from the pack.

I backed down off the rock and watched him turn gracefully on the log, still watching me. Then, like the fish, he was gone with a flick of his tail. We had obviously come to some type of unspoken and unwritten agreement that we would go our own way. Not the first wolf I had ever negotiated with.

I know this will be one of those snippets of memories that never leave, but regretfully I head back up the path. A couple of Jays land on a picnic table and cock their heads expectantly as I approach. A quick search of the truck turns up a potato chip bag with some crumbs. I shake it out on the table and they are gone in an instant. I feel better giving something back

Pulling back out on the highway, I leave the music off. My God the trees and cliffs are absolutely gorgeous. Reds, yellows, greens, and some shade of purple vine running up and down the washes. I realize I have missed at least three hours of 'calendar driving' on my record attempt and I feel the guilt again.

Maybe I will get up early Sunday morning. It won't take that long to get back up here. At least that's what McGregor says.

Maybe the Season Won't Change This Year

If you're a student of meteorology or an avid reader of The Farmer's Almanac you are no doubt aware that we have just experienced the Autumnal Equinox. You don't have to be a neighbour of Stonehenge to see that, for a few days, the hours of darkness and sunlight are equal in length. To be more direct, the season has changed; it is now fall.

The challenge this year is that it doesn't seem like fall. The change from summer to autumn in the Lower Mainland is the most dramatic of seasonal transitions. The other season changes are marked only by the change in temperature of the rainwater.

This year I'm not ready for fall to arrive. I'm enjoying walking around in shorts and t-shirts and eating meals on the deck or picnic table. Normally we have dragged out the sweaters and jeans, polished up the boots and pulled the hoodies and jackets from the back of the closet.

The situation is somewhat like waiting for a flight arrival at the airport. We keep checking the time and date, looking out the window and wondering how much longer the delay will be.

The sounds and smells of fall are very distinct and we usually sense the change coming preceded by a cool breeze or an occasional downpour. But this year, the air conditioning is still on and the sunglasses are still handy. Besides, I don't hear anyone complaining about the delayed arrival.

But, I've decided to take a new position. I'm not waiting, watching or listening any longer. I'll take all the sun that nature is prepared to deliver. At least that's what McGregor says.

Jim McGregor

I'm Not Listening

Wind chimes are tinkling softly today,
With a message in that gentle ring;
I don't want to hear
About storms on the way
Or the cold dreary days
They will bring.

Brown leaves try to catch my attention,
Calling without making a sound;
I don't want to hear
About fallen branches
Or raking leaves
That cover my ground.

Canada geese are V-lining south,
Warning with whispering wings;
I don't want to hear
About oncoming seasons,
I know they're not gaggling
About spring.

The poet is writing
About autumn again,
Searching for rust colored words;
I don't want to read about
Pumpkins or frost,
Changing trees, or south flying birds.

The season will change
If I listen or not,
Let me enjoy one last fall afternoon;
Lately it seems, seasons are shorter,
And they're coming and going
Too soon!

Collecting Memories

I've been collecting stuff lately. The best thing about the stuff I've been bringing home is that I don't have to put it anywhere; it's all stored away in my memory banks. I have a theory that if you fill the shelves in your mind with good stuff, you eventually have to take the bad memories out and throw them away.

This amazing weather has truly aided in my treasure hunting. Two weeks ago, I took my old pick-up down to Fire Hall # 5 to a car show. It's only a few blocks away so the engine didn't even get warm. The Firefighters were raising money for Alzheimer's and the end of the season car show was a huge success.

The lot was full and the gates were opened to the small field at the rear of the property. A dozen or so vehicles were parked down there in a perfect fall scene with orange maple leafs tumbling down onto shiny red or black paint jobs.

I sat in my lawn chair in front of my truck and listened to conversations about tire sizes and horsepower. The smell of frying onions and hamburgers mixed with warm leather upholstery wafted in and out on a cool breeze. I tipped my cap back and sat for a while with the sun on my face and locked away the sights, sounds and smells of this late September day.

Last week I was helping out at the Cranberry Festival in Fort Langley. In the morning dark we were setting up tables and chairs, putting up barricades and setting out traffic cones. The streets are empty and quiet at that time but soon the vendors arrive and set up.

By nine-o-clock the crowds start arriving and it is truly gratifying to stand at the front of the community hall and watch the festival appear before your eyes. By two o'clock we have sold seventy-five hundred pounds of fresh cranberries. The main street and side roads that were so quiet before dawn are now choked with thousands of people.

In the late afternoon I found a quiet bench and sat down with a cup of hot coffee. The kid's stage was off to one side and I could hear the laughter of the children being entertained by a juggler on stilts. Live country music was coming from the main stage across the square and I could recognize the voices of some of my song-writing friends.

Cranberry sausages cooking at the Freybe's tent were blending with the familiar Kettle Corn smell. People carried fresh bread and pies past where I was sitting and conversations varied from pickles and honey to candles and fudge.

I tipped my cap back and sat for a while with the sun on my face and locked away the sights, sounds and smells of this early October day. I found myself thinking about Thanksgiving and how much I was thankful for.

Even as I write this, I am outside in my backyard on Thanksgiving Sunday and I can smell turkey cooking from somewhere. I am writing in the shade but the sun is beckoning to come and sit for a while. If I do, I won't get anything done today.

But all I really have to do is move some of those old memories off the shelf and replace them with better ones. That's best done from a lawn chair in the sun. At least that's what McGregor says.

Mothers and Mother Nature

There were some interesting conversations taking place in homes throughout the Lower Mainland this week. "Honey, do you where my umbrella is? I thought it was in the hall closet but it's not and need it today."

"I haven't seen it but I need a long sleeve shirt and can't find any and my heavy socks are missing too."

"Mom where are my boots, it's raining and I need my boots!"

Yes, the rain blew in overnight and caught everyone by surprise and by noon on the first wet day we were already complaining about how cold and damp it was.

I was at an outdoor event, hunched up trying to keep the rain from sneaking down my neck. The varied state of dress around me illustrated how confused we all were. One guy was wearing shorts and sandals but had a bright yellow Gortex hoody shielding him from the weather.

The ever-present west coast jogger zoomed by, her red legs being punished by the stinging rain and her ball cap pulled down covering the top half of her face.

A lady walked past layered in a sweater, and a windbreaker accessorized by matching scarf and gloves. Her umbrella matched her boots and she was prepared for the worst. However the young boy following her looked like a drowned rat. His soaking wet soccer shirt hung down past his waist, sticking to the mud on his shorts. You could hear his socks squishing in his boots and his teeth were chattering. His wet hair was plastered to his head. Their walk was quiet until he sneezed. That evoked a string of "motherisms".

I couldn't hear exactly what his mother was saying but I'm sure it was those words mothers have been saying for years. "I can't believe you didn't bring a jacket. You're going to catch your death of cold. This is ridiculous to play games in this weather. You'd better not get sick and miss any school. Clean your boots, don't track any mud in the car. You get into a bath as soon as you get home."

Mother's don't have to practice those phrases, they come naturally and instinctively and her warnings will change with the seasons. Last month they included applying sunscreen and not breaking your neck on the trampoline. When the snow comes she'll add the winter cautions about thin ice, throwing snowballs at your little sister and keeping your gloves or mittens on so you don't freeze your fingers off.

Obviously, many adults have forgotten the childhood warnings. The newscasts report an increase in accidents as soon as the rain begins. Drivers have just forgotten the motherly advice to 'slow down and pay attention to what you are doing.'

They are ignoring mom's orders to 'wait your turn, don't push in line and be polite.'

The seasons change and global warming brings about unpredictable weather patterns. But the pre-school lectures will never change and their messages stay with us forever. Admit it folks, before you go out, you hear your mom's voice and you put on clean underwear. If you get a cold or the flu, at some point in your recovery you will have at least one bowl of chicken soup. You will tell you kids to stop running in the house. You can't help it.

Winter is coming. Listen to your mom. Bundle up and keep warm. At least that's what McGregor says.

A Break in the Storm

Is anyone else as surprised as I am that November is here? I suppose when you have an extended summer you expect the rest of the months and seasons to stretch out a bit as well. But the rain is back and the winds are rattling the windows so, ready or not, it's November.

Last Sunday we had our annual family gathering to celebrate my daughter's birthday and supply the grandkids and nieces and nephews with their Halloween pumpkins. Even though Grandpa doesn't grow the pumpkins anymore it is still a lot of work for him to drive to the pumpkin patch, load them, unload and spread them around in the garden so it looks like he grew them.

It had rained steady for two days and I was prepared for the worst. But on Sunday morning the sun was shining and the rain held off all day. Everyone spent the afternoon outside, and as the adults reminisced about Halloweens gone by, the kids jumped and ran and threw balls and the dogs raced around the yard endlessly. A lot of pent up energy was released.

It was an easy afternoon with lots of laughs and a chocolate cake with candles to mark another year gone by. I learned things about my kids I never knew as some old trick or treat stories were dusted off. I was surprised to find out they weren't the angels I had thought they were. A large flock of geese flew over and I learned that the reason one line of the V is always longer is because there are more geese in that line. An informative fall day for sure.

We made the most of the break in the storm. There is a good lesson there because we were never promised a calm passage, just a safe harbour. Maybe our storm is a hurricane gathering strength in our personal life, and if we take some time, take a break away, the worst will blow over.

When we see a glimmer of sunshine in those dark clouds, that's the time to re-stock, refresh and gather strength for the next heavy weather that is bound to arrive. We've all watched and listened to the earthquakes and hurricanes around us this week and here we sit, quiet and safe in the middle; in the break in the storm.

I recall walking through a Tofino rainforest during a torrential downpour and not realizing the rain had stopped until I realized how quiet it had gotten. Look for the peace and quiet during the breaks in storms of your life. At least that's what McGregor says.

Jim McGregor

Break in the Storm

It stopped!
I hadn't noticed the break in the rain
Until the gulls appeared again;
Out from their shelter to swoop and soar,
Their cries swept away by the ocean's roar;
They glide on currents pulling clouds apart,
Exposing a canvas for West Coast art.

But God!
Close your eyes and breathe the air,
Let the salt spray strip your senses bare;
Smell the forest, the moss, the sea,
Hear the raindrops slip from tree to tree;
Take a seat, relax, watch nature perform,
It's just intermission, a break in the storm.

Thanks for All the Little Things

I was waiting for inspiration for a column. You have to wait for the idea to come; you can't force it. The ideas are all around like airwaves but you have to be set on the right frequency for them to come blasting in.

My problem was that I had been thinking this weekend was Thanksgiving and maybe that should be my topic. Now, nothing else is coming in but Thanksgiving. Playwright Noel Coward explains," Writing is easy, get a pen and paper and start to think very hard. After a while, drops of blood appear on your forehead and the words come shortly after."

I decide get my mind off it and go grocery shopping. A quick check of the fridge shows I have a bunch of leftovers to throw out. Uneaten meat and vegetables go into the recycling or the compost. I scoop up my money off the dresser and head out, making a note to go to the bank machine.

It is a cool fall day but on the weekend I bought a new lined jacket and it seems perfect for the day.

I see the gas prices have dropped so I decide to fill up. A full tank still comes to $100.00 but I have my pensions and some part time work so I can afford the gas as it fluctuates up and down. Still nothing comes to help with the column.

In the grocery store I meet a buddy who has been struggling with health issues. He's on the mend but still has a way to go. He has had a tough year financially and emotionally as well. I have been able to keep my weight down and keep active and I feel pretty good. Too many guys I retired with are either sick or gone. I guess I'm lucky.

I fill up the cart with things I need and some I don't need. There is a great price on turkeys today. I will probably get a couple of invites for Thanksgiving dinner, maybe I can write about family gatherings but I've already done that.

I will probably take my Mom over to my sister's for dinner or my daughter is a great cook and always has a big meal. With any luck, one will be having it on Sunday and the other on Monday and I can get to both. On top of that I always buy my own small bird to cook so I'll have something here at home to pick on. No ideas for the column yet.

On the way home, the wind and rain have picked up and as I pull in the driveway I'm glad I put the new roof on last spring and fixed the gutters. Lots of storms to come and nobody likes a leaky roof.

I sit down at the computer. My thoughts have been all over the place. Food in the fridge, money in the bank, warm clothes, good health, reliable transportation, friends and family close by, warm and dry shelter and maybe two

Thanksgiving meals. All this running through my mind but no inspiring thoughts about Thanksgiving. The answer is close but I can't put my finger on it.

What if I'm looking for a big answer to the big picture when all I really have to do is get down on my knees and say thanks for all the little things? Happy Thanksgiving, at least that's what McGregor says.

Bring the Sunshine with You

There was a friendly buzz in the coffee shop. Customers shared conversations and a few laughs and the two girls behind the counter giggled at something on their phones. Everyone seemed to be in a good place.

When the bell over the door tinkled, one of the girls looked up and said, "Oh no, it's him again." I looked at the elderly gentleman that had walked through the door and was headed for the counter. He seemed oblivious to the people around him and if the scowl on his face wasn't permanent, it appeared to have been there for a very long time.

He looked at the blackboard sign then barked, "If that is the special it is not special to the customers at those prices." The girl asked what she could get him. "I'll have a coffee and the soup and sandwich special, if the soup is hot today, last time it was just lukewarm." The girl rang up his order, took his money and made change that he pocketed, leaving no tip.

"Here is your coffee, we'll bring your order out to you."

"No," he replied, "The last time you forgot and it sat on the counter and got cold. I'll wait here for it." He stood rigidly at the counter not giving ground to other customers who had to manoeuvre around him. He got his lunch and sat by himself.

He had changed the whole atmosphere in the room. The girls were nervous and upset, conversation in the room had become subdued and when he was finished he pushed his chair back with a loud scrape and stalked out. I said a quick prayer for him because it seemed he hadn't been taking time to say one for himself.

What happens when you walk into a room? Are people happy to see you walk in or are they happier to see you walk out? Do you drop the temperature in the place or do you bring in a bit of sunshine?

I used to think people were glad to see me coming and be cheered up until I had my roast recently. Apparently, according to the 'roasters', I have once or twice inadvertently told the same joke a few times to the same people. Words like tedious, obnoxious and tiresome were bandied around and apparently laughing at the Chief's jokes was the only way to get promoted.

But I didn't care what they were saying about me because the people in the room were laughing and having a great time and we were raising money for a good cause. If they're laughing with me or laughing at me, what does it matter if the result is positive?

I had a former artist partner who was trying to teach me to read auras. She explained in detail that a person's aura was a different color depending on their mood, but try as I might, I couldn't see any halos around people's heads. She could tell if people were dishonest or sad or if they were sending out positive energy. A great tool if we could all do it. I just tell them a joke, if they laugh they are well adjusted. If they don't, they are probably suffering from some deep internal trauma.

That man in the coffee shop hadn't laughed for a very long time. If you want to live longer, bring the sunshine into the room with you. At least that's what McGregor says.

It Was a Dark and Stormy Night

We were all prepared for the storm and went whizzing right by us with nary clap of thunder, nor a flooded street. Most of us were relieved, but I'm sure some school kids had counted on getting a couple of days away from school and the weather forecasters are busy wiping the egg from their faces.

For the most part we heeded the warnings and cleaned our eaves troughs and driveway drains. We fuelled up our cars, we stocked up our shelves and we charged up our cell phones and laptops. We shored up our beaches and piled up our sand bags. We bought batteries and candles and put away our patio furniture. But nothing happened.

It reminded me of the story of Canadian heavyweight boxer who had been struggling in his last few bouts. In preparation for his next fight, he trained daily for six months. Jogging, biking, sparring, on the road and in the gym and entered the fight in the best athletic shape of his life. He knocked his opponent cold in less than three minutes of the first round.

After the fight he told his manager, "The fight didn't even last three minutes. What a waste of time all that training was!"

We are not used to hearing words like typhoon, cyclone, tornado or hurricane in our forecasts. Those are East Coast words reserved for far away countries, so they spurred us into action and now we are probably better prepared for the winter than we normally are at this time of year.

I'm sure there are many strategy meetings in the newsrooms as to how they are going to cover such catastrophic events. No doubt the reporters on the lower end of the scale draw straws to see who is going to be sent out to Tsawwassen to stand in the gales and rain on the Ferry terminal and risk a rogue wave or a mighty gust tossing them out into the storm tossed Pacific surf.

It must be annoying when the anchor back in the studio is sipping hot coffee while they are asking them to describe the scene. Then, just as the wind - blown reporter regains her balance and continues to report how dangerous it is and how important it is to stay away from the area, three wind surfers glide past her in the background waving at the cameras. We west coasters don't take life or storms too seriously.

We are always going to have storms in our life. Emotional storms, physical storms, family storms, and friend storms. To survive them we have to fuel up and keep energized, stay healthy and prepared for the day-to-day tornados and floods of crisis.

We have to shore up our foundations and keep the faith. We have to surround ourselves those that can be our buffers and keep life from rising over our heads and dragging us down, the people we can cling to when the sky gets dark and the gales get too strong.

Most of all, we can't base our life on the people who always say the sky is falling, the people who tell us we are doomed. Every storm passes.

Buy the batteries and the candles when the sun is shining and build your friendships when the times are good. They'll all come in handy when the power goes out and the times get tough. Be prepared. At least that's what McGregor says.

Taking it Slow

I have come to appreciate a slower pace. It's nice when I don't have to set the alarm clock, rush through breakfast and put on tight shoes. I like it when I can rub my hand across my chin and make a conscious decision whether I should shave or not today. If I'm just going to be alone in my home office all day, maybe even a shower is optional.

It's also nice when the season makes a gradual, calm transition as well. This last weekend, fall just seemed to stroll in quietly, standing off in the corner at first so we barely noticed it was here. No rush to scatter leaves across the lawn or dump chilly rain, just stretching and yawning and dragging a few clouds across the sky, not quite ready to go to work yet.

Everyone seemed to be aware that this might just be one of the last nice weekends and they were out in the parks and the playgrounds. This is was a teaser weekend that grabs first time soccer families and pulls them in.

As the parents sit in their lawn chairs in shorts, sweaters and sunglasses they watch their kids running up and down the field in the fresh air and sunshine, outside with other kids and they are happy they made the decision to get their kids involved. They relax in the fall sun and meet and chat with other new parents.

They have no idea that six weeks from now, the rain will be blowing horizontally across that same field and the accompanying wind will be sucking the heat from their thermal mugs and no attempt at layering clothing will keep them warm. But the kids won't care and they will still be outside in the fresh air.

The perfect mix of sun and clouds on this first fall weekend was an invitation to walk, jog, picnic, or start winterizing the yard. Should I take the cushions off the patio furniture or maybe wait a bit and take the old truck to the last car show of the year at the High School?

We'll all be hunkered down soon enough so don't waste the good days. At least that's what McGregor says.

Jim McGregor

A Day at the Park

Wheel chairs, roller blades, sandals, sneakers,
Barefooted giggling hide and seekers;
Dog feet chasing 'cross the lawn,
No one sees the leash is gone.

Food spread out on picnic tables
All homemade treasures, no store labels,
Some relaxing in the sun,
Some have come to bike or run.

Rolling, strolling, sleeping, eating,
Tai Chi, talking, writing, reading;
Busy day from dawn 'til dark,
An Autumn Sunday in the park.

Slipping Into the Landscape

Have you ever looked at a painting of a beautiful landscape or a lake scene and noticed that the artist has slipped in a small image of a person walking on a trail or maybe gliding across the calm water? The image appears that it has been included almost as an afterthought. Maybe it's there to give the painting some perspective, defining the size of the trees or the expanse of the scene. Possibly, it is wishful thinking on the artist's part. Has he been there on that trail, crossing that lake or maybe he just wants to be.

We don't always get to choose the landscape we appear in every day. If we are in the rush hour traffic, nose to tail, stopped with a thousand of others we wish we were anywhere else and we examine the circumstances that placed us in this scene. Maybe we're here for financial reasons on the way to work. Maybe we have an appointment to keep.

If we have been sketched into a cubicle with piles of work on our desk we might question why the artist didn't at least give us a window or a quiet studious neighbour. If our surroundings include hospital beds with drab walls we wonder why we were put in this scene instead of being placed in the canoe on the lake.

All these thoughts filtered through on one of the many of the amazing autumn days we've just enjoyed. How many did you waste? How many hours were you able to steal and slip out of your abstract scene into a picture perfect fall day? We never do it often enough, we don't play as much as we should and we spend too much time looking out the window at the leaves falling and not enough time listening to them crunch under our feet.

Nasty weather is coming so find a scene to your liking and phone in sick. At least that's what McGregor says.

Watercolour

I've been brushed into a painting
In a field in late September,
An artist's concept
Of an early autumn scene.
He has put away the mixes
For the summer shades of landscapes
And has painted every other hue than green.

He has me sitting on a log
Beneath a maple that's exploded
Into fifty-seven different shades of brown.
My feet are hardly visible
Under deep and crunchy leaves
And He even has a couple floating down.

For grass He has decided,
A sandy desert shade will do
With an oasis of some brambles here and there;
For sky He's chosen a concoction
That I'll call October blue
And He's somehow painted crispness in the air.

Just behind me is a black Lab
In a perfect hunter's point
As a frightened pheasant breaks to fly away;
How fortunate I am
The Painter chose me as his subject
And placed me in this picture perfect day!

Jim McGregor

Jack Frost

It was nice to wake and see the lawn covered with frost instead of puddles. Whenever that happens, I am reminded of the philosophical words of Red Green: "The first frost of the year covered the windows. The morning sun sparkled through in shapes of diamonds and stars; no one could see in, I could not see out. I wasn't worried though, I had driven this road many times!"

Yes, we've all seen them haven't we? The drivers who refuse to scrape the windows before venturing forth. There are various types of non-scrapers. We find some who can't wait for the defrosters and leave when they have a small strip to view through the steering wheel just above the dashboard. Driving with one hand, they have become experts at holding their steaming coffee cup up to the glass to assist the fan.

Then there is the guy whose Visa card has been over the limit for a year but he still carries it so he can use it as an ice scraper. Usually, he will scratch out a four by six inch slot to see through. Now he can manoeuvre through the neighbourhood like an armoured personnel carrier, peering

272

through the view slot watching for us rebels approaching from the side streets.

There is always at least one driver who will turn on his windshield wipers to the fastest setting, relying on friction and his windshield washer fluid to melt a hole in the frost.

Some drivers will get the windshield clear but not the side or back windows. They drive in a straight line, once in a while flicking on their turn signals and waiting for a horn honk to alert them if anyone else is behind or beside them.

Yes, it is a great time of year for innovations. Drivers in other parts of the country use such aids as block heaters, long handled multi-purpose scrapers or even keep gloves in their glove compartments. We try many different methods.

For instance, instead of lock de-icer, a kettle full of hot water poured over the door handle will get you into your car lickety-split. When scraping, pulling your sleeve down over your hand and then blowing on your fingers to warm them is much quicker than going back into the house to look for your gloves. You'll usually only find one of them anyhow. Unless of course, you yell at someone else to look for them while you are filling the kettle.

Some people are convinced that if, while sitting in your driveway, you turn the defroster on full blast then push down on the accelerator, it will clear faster. Of course these are the neighbours that have to get up an hour and a half before you do.

One evening, when the weatherman said the temperature was going to drop overnight, I decided to be pre-emptive. I went outside and covered my windows with newspaper so I could zip it off in the morning and be on my way in a jiffy. Believe it or not, the weatherman was wrong! It rained all night, the paper returned to its pulp state, and by the time I got the mess peeled off, I had to go back in and change.

It is November, snow and frost and ice are on the way. Gloves and an ice scraper in your glove box are probably a good idea. At least that's what McGregor says.

WINTER

Winter Wonderland

I was taking down some Christmas cards when I came across one with a lovely scene titled, 'Winter Wonderland.' The sun glistened on the new fallen snow as a young couple pulled out of the farmyard in a one horse open sleigh. Mother waved a cheery greeting from the expansive porch and carollers were singing on the corner. Beautiful, but definitely not a Langley Christmas scene.

If it were a local card, the young couple's vehicle would be half in the driveway and half in the crusted ruts on the street. She would be behind the wheel with her foot to the floorboards spraying him with brown frozen muck. Mother would be on the porch on her cell phone yelling at BCAA and the carollers would be singing the Langley version of Winter Wonderland: *In the lane, tires spinning; don't you know winter's winning; you dig all day long 'til a plow comes along, blocking in your driveway once again!*

The novelty has worn off; even the shovelling has lost its effectiveness. Early on we waved and smiled at neighbours as we cleared the driveways down to bare asphalt or concrete.

Now, only the minimum effort is put forth. Maybe a bit at the road or clearing the sidewalks so you don't get another nasty note from the mailman.

The kids are not enjoying the snow anymore. Most of them are upset that all of this came during Christmas vacation. Playing in the snow when school has been cancelled is much more exciting than simply being allowed to "go outside and have fun".

The animals have had enough too. At the first snowfall, dogs rolled and frolicked, jumping high in the air to catch snowflakes and gallop after sticks or balls. After a month they are now wondering what they have done so wrong to be dragged outside to poop on a sheet of ice in the back yard. Cats just sit on the windowsills, their tails twitching as they figure who will pay for being shut in and how bad the punishment will be.

Even the snowmen are tired and showing signs of depression. Just before Christmas a magnificent snowman appeared down the street. He was well over six feet tall, a happy grin under a hat and scarf, two branch arms that waved a cheery hello. But the other night after continuous melting and thawing, I turned the corner and my headlights picked up an eerie sight on their lawn.

He was bent and misshapen; his head had melted to one side and frozen to one shoulder making him look like Quasimodo. His hat and scarf were gone and most of the stones had dropped out, his grin now a sneer. Only one arm remained and it was twisted in a manner that the one remaining twig finger was turned upward in a Trudeau-like salute to the weather. His one remaining eye followed me, begging me to drive into him, smash him and end it all. But after all, he was made of snow and why should he be freed of this misery?

Remember the old Christmases we used to have? The pouring rain, the green lawns, I'm going to start now and produce a line of Langley Christmas cards for next year. Nothing says Langley better than a picture of a four-wheel drive upside down in the median of Highway One. At least that's what McGregor says.

Jim McGregor

Marbles for Christmas

I've been out picking up toys and handing out toys this week. Most of the schools, banks and individual businesses collect toys for the Christmas Bureau and we are more than willing to go get them, bring them in, sort them by age groups and make sure they go to deserving homes.

We have some dedicated volunteer drivers to do most of the toy retrieval, but once in a while, just as I start to tell jokes, one of the ladies will hand me a piece of paper send me off on a pick up. Coincidence, I guess! But I don't mind, because driving around with a truckload of toys for hundreds of boys and girls is as close to being Santa as you can get. I guess you could say I do it because it's a 'clause' in my contract.

We have a tradition with a couple of schools in the City that involves some of our volunteers going to the classroom to talk about the Langley Christmas Bureau and explain our programs to the kids. Our people explain that the toys the kids have brought are going to less fortunate families that otherwise wouldn't have toys under the tree Christmas morning. We feel it is important to show even the youngest in our community that they can make a difference in someone's life.

As the kids bring their toy up to the box, they are asked to tell us what age group they have bought for and a sticky note goes on the toy for sorting. It is a rewarding experience for all but this year the ladies came back with watery eyes as they related an experience during the session at the school.

A grade one boy, about six years old, came up with a small toque. He handed it over and said, "I think this will be good for a baby." Then he rummaged around in his pocket, pulled out a small shiny marble, handed it over and said, "And I think this would be good for a boy about my age."

I think he had been listening, and there behind all the trappings and trimmings of the season, the noise and lights, the hustle and bustle, he found something that meant the world to him, and he gave it away. I do believe that's how this all started many centuries ago.

If I asked you stop reading for a minute and think about the best Christmas gift that you ever received, even you may be surprised what pops into your mind. I also bet it won't be the most expensive gift you ever received either.

I remember getting a Visible V-8 Engine model one year. Once assembled and hooked up to batteries you could see valves and pistons moving and spark plugs light up. But what made it special is that my Dad worked on that model with me, explaining the mechanics as we went along. He was a busy man with a big family, a job, and a farm but for a while we worked together on that model and I got some of his time. I knew how precious that time was to him.

How many precious marbles do you have in your marble bag and how many are you willing to part with? Put a little thought into your gift giving; make them gifts people will remember for years. At least that's what McGregor says.

The Flu

It might have been the damp weather or maybe it was exposure to hundreds of people coughing and sneezing around me, but I came down with the flu. Now let's be clear here, this was man flu and it comes on hard and fast. It starts with a tickle in the back of your throat or maybe a bit of a headache, and the next thing you know, you have difficulty even moving.

The chills set in then the overall aching is followed by back spasms, cramps, nausea and weakness. Probably the closet a woman comes to the pain of man flu is childbirth. Lifting and turning your head is difficult because your hair hurts. Frustration sets in as the numbers on the remote control blur and your fingers barely have strength to push the buttons. A man learns it is no use calling for help, a request for assistance is usually met with a reply such as, "Oh for God's sake, you're not dying you have a bloody cold!"

The only respite here is to phone your mother. She knows you are probably not getting the care you need and will tell you to 'get plenty of rest, drink lots of fluids and just take it easy.' But taking it easy for a man is a hard task indeed because the man flu carries with it a deep psychological factor that creates mental anguish in combination with the physical pain. It is not normal for man to sit back and let others lead.

This urge to get up and provide at all costs goes back to the dawn of time itself. In the prehistoric societies, man was the hunter, the gatherer. If he were not able to throw the spear or swing the club it could spell disaster for the family unit or even the entire clan. This ribbon of DNA has wound its way into the very fibre of every modern man and instinctively he knows he has to provide and protect for his family unit. To simply lie there and 'take it easy' causes as much pain as the high temperature that now sears its way through his weakened body.

The potential for someone to harness the man flu bug for terrorism use is as great as that danger from Anthrax or some other exotic virus. Consider this scenario. A terrorist cell somehow infects all the males of a country with the man flu at the same time. They wait twenty-four hours, and then they simply drive quietly into the capitol building or parliament, no weapons, no battles. They walk up to the heads of state or military commanders who are all sitting huddled over steaming mugs of Neo-Citron, stinking of Vicks vapo-rub and they quietly say, "We're here to take over your country." The ailing men would simply say, "Go ahead, the keys are on the hook by the door, just leave me alone." No loss of life no destruction of property, just taking advantage of a terrible weakness.

But to all my faithful readers, there is no need to send cards or get well wishes for I have come through the darkness. As I sit here, my hands cupped around a bowl of chicken noodle soup, the golden elixir is sending strength back to my muscles and before long, I will be chasing the sabre-toothed again. I am man and I will prevail, At least that's what McGregor says.

Get Ready for the Season

I had to stop as the large flat deck truck pulled slowly off Production Way onto Fraser, taking all the lanes in the process. As I pulled beside him I noticed that from the "headache rack" to the taillights, the trailer was loaded with pallets on which hundreds of 10kg containers of Sifto Salt were piled six high. I was surprised there weren't two grizzled old cowboys with shotguns sitting atop the load.

We've seen it before: a hastily made detour sign directs the truck off the highway on to a rural road. The driver rounds the corner to find a fir tree blocking his way. As he stops, disgruntled Brookswood residents drop from the trees and disable the guards while the rest pillage the load, throwing pails of salt into SUVs, sedans and pick-up trucks. Later, the guards will describe them as "crazed".

If we can believe the weatherman, and, I don't know why we wouldn't, by the time you are reading this, it is warmer and raining and most of the ice and snow is gone. We all got caught because the storm came on New Year's Eve. Nobody had to go anywhere for two days, workers were off, and we all expected the weather to turn to rain and slush and wash away like it usually does, but it froze. Mother Nature obviously does not pay attention to Statutory Holidays.

Then when we went to get salt to melt it, they were out. One hardware employee told me that he has noticed that the folks coming in for salt in January are the same ones that get annoyed because there are no fans in August. This month, the salt supplies will be replenished and nobody will rush to buy it.

We're good shovellers in our neighbourhood. The driveways get cleaned as soon as the snow stops and we keep on top of it. Often we gather at the end of the driveways, take a breather, lean on our shovels and discuss snowplows, assessments, politics or other things we have absolutely no control over, and it becomes an event.

With four boys in the house, my Dad never came home from work to a snow-covered driveway. Nobody told us to go out and shovel, it was understood. Even when his heart and hips slowed him down, we did our driveway then went over did his. Most times we were rewarded with hot coffee and muffins or cookies just out of the oven. It never seemed like work although he did have a homemade plywood shovel that had to be screwed back together at least twice.

In the olden days, you could drive through Langley City after a snowfall and honk and wave at Tony Slogar shovelling in front of the Arcade Barber Shop, Aksel Ebbesson in front of the 5 to Dollar and Laurie King in front of Arnold and Quigley. Sure there was a by-law but they did that for their customers, their neighbours and their employees. Nobody had to threaten them with a fine.

The trouble is, when we live in the land of milk and honey, when we awake in the morning we want milk and honey and nothing less, especially if we have to do a bit of work for it.

Buy salt in August and fans in January and you'll be set for the year. At Least that's what McGregor says.

Memories in the Smoke

There is something special about a campfire on a cold December day. The good folks at Township 7 Winery invited the Christmas Bureau people to put up a toy collection box at their Open House last weekend. The day was spectacular and the scene was enhanced by a large open fire in their fire pit. The snapping and crackling of the dry fir logs attracted folks with their wine glasses outside into the sun.

There are no strangers around a campfire. It is almost impossible to stand there quietly without a conversation breaking out. It starts innocently enough. "We should have some spuds wrapped in foil to stick in those coals," says one person. Then a Maritimer adds, "And a lobster pot over the flames would be a nice touch." Another lady chimes in, "We had fires at Grandpa's farm that burned all day and well into the night when we were kids."

The lowly wiener becomes a feast fit for a king if it's cooked properly over the coals, turning slowly and blistering evenly. Slathering the finished product with ketchup, mustard and relish provides the finishing touch that makes enduring the smoke all worthwhile.

Dancing with the campfire smoke is an art in itself. Some will say the smoke follows them no matter where they stand. Others will swear that if you repeat, "I hate white rabbits," three times, the smoke will shift. It doesn't really matter because at the end of day, your jeans, your jacket and your hair will smell of smoke, a nice reminder of the day.

As the Christmas carols drift across the field, conversation turns to our favourite Christmas song. The debate pits old crooners like Sinatra and Crosby against newcomers like Bieber and Buble. Which is better, the original Christmas Song by Mel Torme or the Nat King Cole version? Is Anne Murray's Christmas special still the best or have newcomers replaced her?

The younger people are looking at each other, trying to be polite and not mention that they've never heard of any of these folks. One of them pulls out a device that looks like Captain Kirk's communicator, pushes some buttons and starts playing some of the old favourites we've been discussing.

The fireside conversation moves on to Christmas movies and TV shows. Is Alistair Simms's Scrooge better than Bill Murray's? Is Tom Hanks in The Polar Express better than Burl Ives in Rudolph? Is Chevy Chase better in Christmas Vacation than Jimmy Stewart in It's a Wonderful Life?

The afternoon lingers in the sun and new people come out as others wander away. The conversations pour out like smooth chardonnay and in the smoke we see ghosts of Christmas past and spirits of Christmas yet to come.

As the community grows we lose the ability to gather around the fire. I recall the conflicts in the City as the old houses came down and the apartments went up. Instead of neighbours coming out to talk around the fire in a homeowner's back yard, the 2nd.floor tenants next door would phone the fire department and complain about the smoke. Eventually the complaints won out and the fires were banned, and the neighbours never met.

Now a whole generation will never know the meaning of the song, 'Chestnuts roasting on an open fire." But, when Jack Frost is nipping at your nose, you can't beat a good fire. At least that's what McGregor says.

Neighbours Don't Need Help

While watching a college a football game, the suggestion was made that possibly I would like to go help my neighbour to put up his Christmas lights and then he might come and help me put up mine.

There are two problems with that theory. First, there was an assumption that I had some ambition to put up my Christmas lights. You don't just decide on the spur of the moment to put up your lights. There is the untangling and testing and replacing of bulbs that are all part of a pre-planning process and this has to take place first.

Secondly, no guy goes over to another guy's yard and asks to help him with anything, particularly putting up his lights, because every homeowner has a 'system' unique to his personality. For instance, some guys will be up on the ladder with a tape measure and a small level handy in their tool belt. They will make sure there is exactly the same spacing between each bulb and that the light wire stays level with the eves. When the lights are up, he will walk out on the street and ensure that everything is symmetrical.

His neighbour, however, may be the type of guy that attacks his house with a staple gun and is more concerned with how quick he can put the lights up rather than how good they look. These two guys could never work together. All it would take would be for one neighbour to say, "Seriously, does that look straight to you?" and the Christmas spirit disappears.

Most men enjoy the solitude of being up on the ladder, surveying their property from on high and contemplating the upcoming Christmas season, the parties, the shopping, and the family gatherings. This may be his last quiet time.

The last thing he wants is a chatty neighbour yattering about the weather, discussing the Grey Cup or speculating on who the Prime Minister is going to apologize to this week.

Even family members trying to help can be a distraction. A well - meaning wife can challenge your manhood when you have to keep saying, "No dear, I am not going to fall off the ladder" or "No honey, I am not going to electrocute myself." It can become tense when the Dad blurts out to his teenage son, "I don't care how cold your fingers are, and you're not going back in to that X-Box until these lights are up."

But it can be a different story if the homeowner invites someone over to help him because he will usually choose someone who can take orders, be quiet, and work until the job is done, like one of his employees or a brother-in-law that owes him money.

The best reward you can give your neighbour is simply to say, "Your lights look great, Bob." He will reply, yours too, Jim, Merry Christmas." That's how you stay great neighbours. At least that's what McGregor says.

Care and Caution

It seems recently we have seen an increase in the number of tragic and devastating fires on the newscasts. Winter brings along many challenges for residents to heat older homes and people start using fireplaces that haven't been used for months or adding space heaters to those draughty basement rooms.

The Christmas season encourages everyone to add lights, trees and candles to enhance the spirit and we entertain more, stay up later, and drink a bit more and maybe just get a bit more careless than usual.

For many years I sat on Building and Fire Code Committees. We would work diligently to bring about National or Provincial regulations that would make homes more fire resistant, buildings stronger to withstand storms and be still standing after earthquakes.

We would study fires and collapses and experiences from across the country and we would recommend changes to construction standards and promote the use of safer interior finishes and upgraded heating and cooking systems.

It was our goal to ensure that the dwellings being built, whether single family homes or multi-family complexes, were safer than they had ever been.

Then we did the worst thing we could do to these new homes. We allowed people to move into them. Furnace rooms became storage closets. Holes were poked in firewalls to run computer cables or phone lines through. Extension cords and power bars were run behind couches or under rugs and they cursed the stupid breakers that kept going off and had to be reset. Barbecues sprang up on combustible balconies next to vinyl siding and fireplaces were stuffed with unseasoned wood and newspaper. Slowly, many of the life saving features built into the home were simply bypassed by the homeowner.

I hated investigating house fires. The smell of wet, crumbling Gyproc, melted plastic and smouldering furniture made me physically sick. It always meant, pain, sorrow and loss. It was often easy to spot the point of origin of the blaze and having to point out to the homeowner who or what was responsible for the fire was never an easy task.

It was never easy to stand in someone else's living room and trace the fire from the Christmas tree to the drapes, across the ceiling and onto the new Lazy-boy. Even harder to see Grandpa's clock knocked from the mantle and smashed on the floor or the family Bible, open to the Christmas story, scorched and trampled into the melted carpet and the toys in the kid's rooms destroyed beyond recognition.

Then, one of the firefighters from outside would say, "The homeowner's just pulled up." That was not the time for blame or to discuss cause, that was a time for consolation and to hear the questions about the whereabouts of family pets or valuable documents, photographs or jewellery. With every recent newscast, the smells, those questions and their tears all come back in an instant.

So many times the cause could have easily avoided, just a little more care, a little more common sense. A visit from an electrician to put in another outlet or two, a regular check of the furnace, a call to a chimney cleaner or a regular clean-up of junk and debris can save a lot of tears. Working smoke alarms and sprinklers do save lives.

Houses are built safer today than ever, don't you be the biggest hazard in your family's home. At least that what's McGregor say.

Scots!

Aye, and a fine Robbie Burns Day to you all! Yes, in January, people of Scottish heritage set aside a day to celebrate the birthday of that infamous Scottish poet, which gives them permission to do all kinds of things that day that they do every other day of the year for no reason at all.

I shouldn't restrict it to those of Scottish heritage for we all become Scots on Robbie Burns Day. We all wear green and 'Kiss me I'm Irish' buttons on St. Patrick's Day, and we all sport a maple leaf of some sort on Canada Day. Canadians just like to have a reason to celebrate so we'll jump on any bandwagon going by and march in the next parade coming down the street.

This was much in evidence at a Burns Dinner I was asked to MC last week. You name the nationality and it was represented there, all raising funds to send the White Spot and Greighlan Crossing Pipe bands to Glasgow next summer. These are kids from eight to eighteen on the way to a World Championship. It was a great evening of dancing, piping, drumming, scotch tasting, poetry, and singing. It was the kind of evening Burns himself would have shelled out money to attend.

There was a fine steaming haggis piped to each table by the band. Some relish the spicy, delicacy and devour huge mouthfuls while others are too sheepish and just don't have the guts. I particularly enjoy the evening as I get to wear my kilt without ridicule. When I got my kilt, I never realized how many different types there were. They even had a James Bond kilt; the sporran was actually a machine gun, very effective but the recoil certainly brought tears to your eyes.

I don't wear the kilt too often because I'm bow legged. Actually, my brother and I are bow legged and my sister is knock-kneed, if we stand in a straight line we spell OXO.

There were a couple of old timers there, Jock and Angus. I heard Angus say he'd been stripping wallpaper all day. I asked if he was redecorating.

"No," he replied, "If an Englishman is stripping wall paper he's redecorating, if a Scotsman is stripping wallpaper he is moving."

They were talking about when God was creating Scotland. Jock said, "He gave us the most beautiful place on earth. Majestic crags for soaring eagles, rivers full of salmon, heather covered hills, clear lochs and vibrant meadows, rocky coasts and hidden valleys."

"Did He not think the others would be jealous? Angus asked. "Aye, He did, so look what he gave us for neighbours!"

Even if you're born in Langley, if you're of Scottish heritage it is the terrible history of Scotland that burns in the blood when the pipes begin to wail. Sir Walter Scott comments, "I am a Scotsman; therefore I had to fight my way into the world." In Arthur Herman's book, *How the Scots Invented the Modern World*, he writes: "being Scottish is more than just a matter of nationality or place of origin or clan or even culture. It is a state of mind."

What's that you say? This column is just a collection of Scottish jokes and author's quotes. Maybe it is, but it didn't cost you a cent, and on Robbie Burns Day, that's a bonny thing indeed. At least that's what McGregor says.

The Fog

I am very upset with the City and Township for their lack of fog removal. For two weeks, we were socked in, blanketed, submerged in a thick cloud and no one from either municipality was making any attempt to clear it away. You only had to drive ten minutes to Abbotsford or White Rock and you would find clear skies, bright sunshine and warm temperatures. Obviously, these are cities that have pro-active fog removal policies in place.

It was dangerous to drive around our community and my calls to the engineering departments were met with either silence or laughter, not a good way to treat a taxpayer. At the very least, they could have called a public meeting to 'clear the air.'

But all joking aside, the fog is not as bad as it used to be. Decades ago, the Fraser River from New Westminster to Mission, was dotted on each side with sawmills. Each of these mills had at least one bee hive burner that smoked all day long. The purpose of these huge furnaces was to dispose of sawdust and mill ends, left over from the mill processes.

On good days, the smoke would dissipate up into the atmosphere. But if a temperature inversion settled over the lower mainland, that smoke just added to any off shore clouds that might roll in, and it was thick.

In addition, most of the homes and businesses relied on wood, coal, sawdust or furnace oil for heat and cooking. I can recall our old house in Otter with a big furnace bin in the basement. The truck from Langley Fuels would come and dump a load down the chute into the furnace room. The cook stove had a sawdust hopper attached to the side and the sawdust would be lugged up in pails and fed into the stove. Of course, the colder and damper it got, the more the stoves and furnaces were used and the thicker the fog became.

There wasn't as much traffic back then but the cars used mostly leaded fuel, which didn't help and headlights were not what they are now so travel was slow when the fog came in. My Dad drove a home delivery milk truck and used to tell us those weeks of fog were more tiring than any other type of driving. He had to drive with the sliding doors open and listen for traffic as he backed in or out of driveways, straining to see some pale lights.

The heavy smogs of those days made it interesting for air travelers. Without today's sophisticated technologies, many flights were diverted from Vancouver International to Abbotsford. As there were no baggage or ticket facilities at Abbotsford, the passengers were bussed back and forth from Vancouver. Imagine trying to do that with today's travelers.

I recall one eventful night when we took Grandma into the airport. The old '56 Chevy didn't go much over 30mph in the fog and the darkness. Grandma and her luggage were plunked on a bus and sent to the plane waiting in Abbotsford. Dad took a wrong turn off the freeway on the way home and we got lost in Surrey. I'm sure Grandma was home in Edmonton before we got back to Langley.

So the next damp foggy day you push the buttons on the thermostat, be glad you're not bringing up a bucket of sawdust. At least that's what McGregor says.

House Cleaning

January and February are pretty boring months. Unless you count Robbie Burns Day and Groundhog Day, there are no reasons to celebrate, no official long weekends. So, when some friends were discussing a reason to get together, I heard myself unexpectedly offering my place, "Come on over," I said.

Then the e-mails started flowing and the visit became an event. A couple of people dropping in is one thing but an event means I should probably make the house presentable. Even though it is just my son and I here we do keep the kitchen clean, the laundry done and the bathroom is respectable should any one drop by, but I was overdue for a good overall scrubbing.

I strolled through the grocery store picking up floor stripper and one step polish for the linoleum, laminate floor spray clean for the laminate and Meadow Fresh carpet deodorizer for the tired old carpets, and a product called Scrub Free for the bathroom and kitchen. I started on the kitchen first.

I decided I'd do the 'deluxe clean' and even pull the fridge out from the wall. Don't ever pull your fridge out. At first I thought there were small dead animals there but they turned out to be large, greasy dust bunnies that required some heavy hands and knees scrubbing. I wrestled the fridge back and then I mopped on the stripper and had to wait until it dried. I was going to make a coffee but I couldn't walk on the floor, not good planning.

I went to the bathroom and decided to do the shower, counter and toilet first, then the floor. I am quick learner. If a product is called Scrub Free one would think no scrubbing is involved. I did the glass shower doors, wiped them down and they were worse. I read the label again and in small red print it said, 'Not recommended for frosted glass doors.' The good old SOS pads did the trick.

With the bathroom done, I went to the kitchen for my coffee. I opened the fridge door and it seems the jostling had moved a carton of milk, which spilled onto the floor. I heard myself say, "Damn, that's my clean floor." That phrase seems to have much more significance when you are the one who has done the cleaning.

Meanwhile the cat was rolling in the Meadow Fresh powder I had sprinkled on the carpet. Not a big deal really, it doesn't hurt a sixteen year old cat to smell meadow fresh once in a while. For most of the day I scrubbed and washed and dusted, and put things away, amazed at how much counter space I have.

The next morning I woke up very uncomfortable. Imagine that, just from doing housework I was stiff and sore! But the place looked great and smelled clean, the company came and we had a great evening.

But as the night wore to a close, my disappointment deepened. I have watched the TV commercials and I know what is supposed to happen. Someone should comment that my bathroom smells 'lemony fresh.' No one mentioned they could see themselves in the shine on my floor. No one rolled on my Meadow Fresh carpets like they were in the great outdoors. Why did I bother? Next time, I'll just spray the place with Spring Rain Febreeze before they come in. At least that's what McGregor says.

Organization

February brings us some interesting mail through our mail slots. Assessments, T-4 slips, charitable tax receipts, all the little reminders that we have to get our tax stuff together. Maybe you are one of those people that are terminally organized and have it all ready to go. I start out like that each year.

A few years back I bought one of those accordion files with folders marked A-Z and some at the back marked Insurance, Bank Statements etc. and each year I start out diligently placing the bills and receipts in the appropriate slots. I can pull out the gas receipts for January, the hydro bill for February, then, it starts to break down. It seems March has a big pile of stuff in there and the rest of the months have very little.

I really was going to get around to sorting it out but at least it's all there. Part of the problem is that I was spoiled when I worked at the Fire Hall. In my office was one big filing cabinet marked 'F'. In there were files on Fire Boots, Fire trucks, Fire Fighters, Fire Budgets, Fire Hose. I think you get the idea. Also, I had a Deputy, an Administrative Assistant, six Captains, numerous Lieutenants and they all seemed very organized and brought me what I wanted when I wanted it. I have none of those people at my house now, hence the lack of organization.

Recently, I listened to a gentleman talk about marketing in the 21st Century. Among other social networking revelations that I will never use, he talked about his "paperless office". It seems he has gotten rid of his metal filing cabinets and desk drawers and has committed everything to the various computer related devices, no more paper. He has documents sent to his hand held device then he forwards them to his scanner, which automatically scans them into the appropriate computer file. How boring! There goes the thrill of looking through piles of paper scattered about your home or office. As you leaf through the documents you find other things you thought were lost. It's like running into old friends. "There you are!" you exclaim.

He showed us how with one touch he can retrieve any phone number instantly. I can too. I speed dial home and after six rings my son answers. I tell him to go upstairs to the kitchen table and get me a phone number written on a brown envelope. "Can it wait?" he asks. We discuss priorities for minute then he finds a brown envelope and shares, "It says Slime and then some scribbles." I tell him it says Steve and the scribbles are numbers. He deciphers my writing and I get the phone number, piece of cake. My son has a way to go before being classed as my Administrative Assistant but then I'm not paying union wages here.

We receive most of our important documents the taxman needs early in the year, but they know there are lots more people like me out there. That is why they give us until the end of April to file, we will have found it all again by then.

I had another column planned for this week but I'll be darned if I know where it is. But I do believe that a clean desk is a sign of a sick mind. At least that's what McGregor says.

Count Your Blessings

It was raining when I went to bed and raining even harder
when I got up. I was warm and dry inside a comfortable home,
a pot of coffee gurgling good morning and homemade stew in
the crock-pot set on low, waiting for lunchtime.

It reminded me of a similar Sunday a few years ago when
my business partner phoned me and asked if I wanted to go
counting eagles. She suggested there might be some good
photo opportunities. After all, we were supposed to be creative
people, always looking for inspiration.

I declined saying I was going to stay home and count
things inside, where it was warm. "What will you count?" she
queried. "Maybe I'll count my blessings," I replied.

We don't do that enough; we spend too much time
counting the raindrops and not the things that really count. I
have been to three memorial services already this year and at
each one, the value of family and friends is front and center,
the people that come through in the tough times.

Determine who the people are in your life that have the
positive influences on you and stay in close personal touch

with them. The people that are still there in your corner during the tough times, they're the ones you can count on. At least that's what McGregor says.

Counting Eagles

I was invited today to go counting eagles,
Rewarding, exciting, they say!
But this is not quite the weather
To number each feather,
I'm not counting eagles today.

I realize they're an endangered species,
But then, my God, aren't we all!
It makes no sense to go
Out in four feet of snow,
To endanger myself with a fall!

I think that today, I'll do other counting,
Go places I haven't been for a while;
Like where each day we live
With much thanks to give,
And thanks never goes out of style!

My first thanks today, will be for my blessings,
So many, just where do I start?
For the talent God gave me
To see what others don't see,
To search with my soul and my heart!

My family today, count them and count on them,
They're there if I want them or not;

Imagine those on their own
Solving problems alone,
Start counting the shoulders I've got!
Count my friends up today, how rich I've become,
Some are new, some I've had quite a while;
I don't need any wealth
If I've got hugs and health,
Someone close to share tears or a smile!

My troubles today, flew off like the eagles,
It seems counting has scared them away;
Bad times I think,
Are soon made extinct,
By counting your blessings each day!

Fitness for the New Year

I planned to write a column on fitness for the New Year. The first challenge is getting my butt off the couch to go get my laptop. We tend to plunk down anywhere soft at this time of year and as long as we are in arm's reach of some food, we are pretty comfortable.

Then suddenly, at about the same time as the Christmas decorations are gone, the peanuts, the butter tarts, the shortbread and the chocolates disappear. That is an indication that the calendar page has been turned and we are off on a new journey into a new year.

If we watch the TV we see that this also signifies a time for personal change. The ads are about fitness, diets, quitting smoking and drinking, getting back to the gym. They show all these amazingly fit actors who have never had a weight problem in their life doing amazing things, all designed to light a fire under us.

I joined a gym once. For twenty minutes I twisted, jumped, bent, and hopped and I still couldn't get those Spandex shorts on, so I went home. Another year I signed up for gym that guaranteed I would lose twenty pounds in thirty days. After thirty days I was the same weight so I phoned to complain. Apparently I was actually supposed to go to the gym during those thirty days. This year, I'm looking at a gym that has a drive through. That sounds promising.

Then there are the diet ads. Following these simple programs seem to be the answer to weight loss. I think the secret is that you go to these places where everyone is as out of shape as you are, or worse, and you just feel better being there with your peers.

I bought a scale for home and I guess one day when I was vacuuming I inadvertently changed it from pounds to kilos. I spent a whole week feeling pretty darn good about well my plan was working. Then I realized what had happened. That can send a guy into depression pretty quick.

Signs are all over. I passed a golf course that had a reader board that said, "I lost twenty golf balls in eighteen holes; ask me how!" A huge guy about three hundred pounds was wearing a t-shirt that said, "I beat anorexia, ask me how!" I once asked a doctor what he thought the best weight loss diet was. "Don't eat anything that tastes good," he replied.

Then of course there are the many types of machines from treadmills to vibrators that will shake calories off your rear end, erase fat from your tummy and increase your heart rate while jiggling loose cholesterol.

I encourage folks who buy these mechanical marvels to use them in the garage. Once you unload them in January, find a spot close to the garage door and use it there. That way when you are selling it at the garage sale in April, it doesn't have to be carried downstairs. Keep the $400.00 price tag on the machine. This is good marketing. When you have it marked "$50.00 OBO", people will know they are getting a great deal.

Don't be discouraged. Sitting on the couch and complaining will get you nowhere. By getting up, moving around, reaching, stretching and bending you will eventually find where she hid those butter tarts. At least that's what McGregor says.

The Time of the Season

The fog lifted and the sun appeared and coaxed me out for a walk one afternoon last week. It felt invigorating to breathe in the crisp air and get my legs moving after moping around the house for a couple of days. I encountered a neighbour and his dog out enjoying the day as well and our discussion turned to Seasonal Affective Disorder.

Seasonal affective disorder (SAD) is a kind of depression that occurs at a certain time of the year, usually in the winter. Symptoms usually build up slowly in the late autumn and winter months and are much the same as with other forms of depression.

This affliction usually occurs in places with long winters or where there have been periods of bad weather that have kept people in doors and socially withdrawn. A good example may be two weeks of steady Langley rain during a hockey lockout. This can bring on many of the signs of SAD; less energy, loss of interest in work, sluggish movements and hopelessness.

It's hard to believe just a lack of sunshine can bring about these changes in personality. It is interesting to note that research shows that SAD occurs more often in women than in men. Now, how many of you guys just said, "Of course, that's her problem lately, Seasonal Affective Disorder, now it makes sense!" Reading this column can be very informative.

Now, just suppose the little lady has been down in the dumps lately. She has been on your case about taking down Christmas lights or doing some random repairs or renovations. She appears unhappy and irritable. Armed with new knowledge about SAD, the next time she starts up simply say, "Hey you grumpy Gus, it sounds like you have Seasonal Affective Disorder. Why don't you put on your boots and coats and mittens and get out in the sunshine and walk those blues away!" You might be very surprised at her reaction.

Further research tells us that SAD was first identified in 1984. I think I'm very glad it wasn't brought to light in the sixties because it can usually start to develop during the teen years. Their symptoms are less energy and the lack of ability to concentrate.

I can see my Dad coming home finding my brothers and I languishing on the couch watching cartoons, and asking, "Why aren't the chores done?" Suppose one of us had answered, "Cut us some slack Dad, we have Seasonal Affective Disorder and we just don't have the energy to complete our tasks." There would have been another type of disorder in the home that would have had a much longer recovery time.

There is a very bright lamp that you can buy that mimics light from the sun. By sitting in front of this for 30 minutes a day your depression will be gone in three or four weeks. It's sort of like when Superman was exposed to Kryptonite and had to retreat to his Dome of Silence for a while. It just takes time.

Couple this news about SAD to another report that tells us that optimistic people have lower blood pressure and healthier enzymes in their blood than those who worry excessively. You have to be a cheerleader.

Belt out a few choruses of *The Sun Will Come out Tomorrow*, tell some jokes, and kick them outside. Your family will thank-you for it. At least that's what McGregor says.

The Attack of the Polar Vortex

The Polar Vortex has stalled over the eastern Provinces again and has frozen the land and the people with its icy grip. I love that term "Polar Vortex". It has great science fiction potential and, not to make fun of the poor folks freezing in Ontario, but I'm sure screen writers are already working on a blockbuster movie.

It will start out with a young female meteorologist just out of university who has been tracking changes in the jet stream. Even though she has detected major changes in the wave patterns and extended severe temperature patterns, no one will listen to her or take her seriously.

The seasoned veterans in their black suits take their glasses off and shake their heads as she speaks before them and wink at each other as they check out her young, shapely legs as she storms out of their offices. (Meteorologists always "storm out!")

Finally, when Canada is covered with ice from coast to coast and oranges start freezing in Florida people start to listen to her. We would have to insert pictures of icicles hanging from the Statue of Liberty and the White House barely visible behind snow drifts. The Prime Minister and the President would call the young lady to appear before them and ask her to find a solution and save the Sochi Olympics because the Russians can't get their act together.

Once she is put in charge she contacts her father's old friends who are former Navy Seals, Green Berets and mercenaries. She brings in Clint Eastwood, Sylvester Stallone, Bruce Willis and Arnold Schwarzenegger and tells them they have to head to the North Pole and reverse the vortex.

They head out in specially designed Hummers with neat tracks instead of tires and of course big machine guns. Along the way they encounter starving rebel forces in Quebec that try to get their supplies. Fortunately Stallone is fluent in French and they get through.

Next they run into herds of savage polar bears that have to be shot and splattered across the ice. Some of the men don't want to harm the endangered species and it causes a rift in the crew. But then one of the hummers slips into a crevice and they have to resort to teamwork to save everyone. Bruce Willis shouts, "We don't leave anyone behind!" They all hug and shake hands and carry on.

Once they get to the North Pole they set up camp smack dab in the eye of the vortex. They open the back of each vehicle and unload two large black boxes. They have brought along a couple of non-tactical nuclear weapons. They are strategically set in place but just as they are set to detonate, one of them starts to slides into the water and we lose Arnold as he sacrifices his life to hold the device steady.

The resulting massive explosion reverses the jet stream. If it was a Canadian movie they would find a passive environmental solution but all American movies must contain a massive explosion somewhere.

The movie ends with American, Canadian, and Russian athletes running abreast carrying their flags toward the opening ceremonies in Sochi. The unknown heroes are in a small, out of the way bar in Nebraska with the young meteorologist, hoisting a drink and toasting Arnold.

"The Attack of the Polar Vortex." Coming soon to a theatre near you. At least that's what McGregor says.

Toques

It was an early January morning; the sky was three different shades of grey meaning that we could either have snow or bright sunshine anytime during the next half hour. I had nowhere in particular to be, sitting at Horton's with a double-double and not really concerned about the weather at all.

Scattered at the other tables were a few friends and acquaintances. Another fire colleague, a couple of guys I had gone to school with, a guy that used to play Little League ball for me years ago, and a couple of police officers. It was a typical Canadian setting and if Norman Rockwell had been there he would have had his sketch pad out for sure.

The conversations were about cars or hockey, the weather or politics, the grocery store fire or the price of gasoline. It was a comfortable morning. Then a bit of laughter and pointing caught everyone's attention and I turned to see what the commotion was about.

At the counter was a customer wearing a toque made out of grey woollen work socks with two extra socks sewn on like ears. All we needed now was Bob and Doug Mackenzie with a couple of Molson Canadian and the scene would be complete.

Toques have a special place in my heart. Years ago, I was doing a stint on the Paraphernalia Committee for the Fire Chiefs' Assn. It was our function to purchase and sell shirts, jackets, cups etc. with the Fire Chief's Assn. logo on them. One of our committee members decided one year to order toques. Five hundred to be exact; five hundred purple and yellow knit woollen toques with an unreadable logo. Maybe the ugliest headwear around until this guy walked into Horton's.

To compound this questionable purchase, our annual conference was always held in June in places like Penticton, Kelowna or Kamloops. Historically, those communities don't have a demand for knit caps in ninety-degree weather.

We could either pack around eight boxes of toques for the next five years or we could get creative. We cut holes in them and marketed them as tea cozies; we cut them lengthwise, re-sewed them and tried to sell them as golf club covers. We went down to the campground where the old retired Chiefs were having their bocce tournament and passed them off as bocce ball bags. You could get four balls in a bag and we did sell some after the cheap old buggers talked us down to half price.

We came up with countless uses for these white elephants and eventually one year when it snowed in Whistler in June we got rid of most of them. The problem was the fallout from all that creativity. You see, I did my time as Education Chairman, I was Chair of the Building and

Fire Code Committee, and I was on the Awards Committee and the Conference Committee. Do people from that Association remember any of those important contributions? No, I am the Toque Guy. I go to a Fire Chief's function and it is only a short time until someone calls out, "Hey McGregor, got any toques for sale?"

But of all those committees I met more folks and knew more names and had more fun pawning off those ugly things in the summer sun. Laugh if they will but we sold them all and he who laughs last, laughs best. At least that's what McGregor says.

Don't Believe Everything You Hear

Have you noticed that in January there is a marked increase in advertisements for exercise machines, supplements and diet plans, all trying to capitalize on those resolutions we made about reducing weight and getting into shape.

The one constant that appears with each promotion is the small print that says, 'When used in conjunction with regular exercise routines." In other words, you can buy all this stuff but unless you get off your butt they probably won't take off any pounds.

Then there are the confusing and contradictory studies we hear every week. Coffee is bad for you. It is bad for your bones and your kidneys, it increases anxiety and heartburn, and it makes menopausal hot flushes worse, it raises your blood pressure and may lead to premature death.

Yet, another study says coffee is good for you. It can make you smarter, it helps you burn fat, it lowers your risk of type II diabetes, it lowers your risk of dementia, and it's good for your liver and reduces the risk of premature death. It doesn't say who did this study but I'm suggesting it might have been Folger's or Maxwell House.

A glass of red wine every day is good for you. It promotes weight loss, it prevents age decline and memory loss, it has many heart healthy benefits, and it works against cancer cells and promotes long life.

But wait a minute. A more recent study tells us that the former studies were flawed because they never took into account the overall alcohol consumption of the study group. I guess some of the folks thought that if one glass of red wine a day was good for you, then five or six glasses a day would make you healthier than ever, or at least bring you to a place where you didn't really care if you were healthy or not.

Like the lady that wrote to the winery and suggested they start putting enough wine in the bottle for two people so her and her friend didn't empty it so fast.

Red meat and fat will constrict your arteries. For years we were told that fat should not be more than 30% of our daily food intake and now the experts tell us there is no proof that people on low fat diets lose any more weight or are any more healthier than those that love that crisp, brown fat sizzling on the edge of a steak or pork chop.

I received a photo the other day captioned, "I made a salad and I'm eating healthy." The picture attached was a frying pan full of bacon and grease with a sprig of parsley in the middle. If you believe it's a salad, then it's a salad.

From all this, I am taking the advice of my favorite folk singer, John Prine when he tells us to "Blow up your TV and throw away your papers." Probably not something my editor wants to hear but in the early 20th century, heart disease was rare. People ate from their gardens, there were less pollutants in the air and they didn't have large corporations giving them conflicting information. They knew what was healthy and what wasn't.

So have a coffee in the morning, eat a salad for lunch, have a glass of wine with your steak dinner, and go for a walk. Sometimes we're our own worst enemy. At least that's what McGregor says.

Snow From Different Perspectives

When you don't have to go to work and have no deeds to do and no promises to keep, you look at snow from a totally different perspective.

Standing inside my warm house with a hot chocolate in hand, I watched my neighbourhood transform into a magic Christmas card scene. In forty-five minutes, my lawn and landscaping look just as good as the neighbour's.

I recall the first day of snow when I was working in the tire shop as the first white flakes created chaos in the parking lot as people scrambled to buy new snow tires or have their old ones installed. Often, when we had to point out to them that their ten year old snow tires had less tread on them than their summer tires did, we were accused of taking advantage of the situation. The flakes weren't just falling from the sky.

When the first All Season tires were introduced it was assumed that now there was no need for snow tires but we had one overzealous salesmen who didn't quite grasp the concept and he sold the customer six All Season tires, two mounted on extra rims for the winter.

No one in the tire shop looked forward to being soaking wet by coffee time and dog tired after a non-stop ten-hour day. Snow was not magical unless you were the owner working the till and humming, "It's beginning to look a lot like Christmas."

When you don't have to drive in a snowstorm it's nice to just bundle up and go for walk. Last week we went out the day after the storm and took pictures of snow covered tree branches and red berries frozen in ice drops on the bushes.

We came around one corner in the park and found four boys skating on a frozen pond in the old pit. Kids playing hockey outdoors in Langley is truly a rare sight. I can only recall two occasions in my life when Fry's Corner, now 176th and Fraser highway, froze over and we went skating trying to avoid the tufts of grass sticking through the ice surface.

But this day, with nothing but time on our hands, we can watch them glide and listen to skates bite into the ice, the only noise carried across this muffled, soft blanket of white.

But in my fire dept. days, snow and cold weather meant an increase in calls for service. Fender benders or major accidents kept us busy all day and night. People having heart attacks from shovelling or broken limbs from slips resulted in many ambulance assists. They were all that much more difficult to perform when we were slipping ourselves or drivers that refused to slow down skidded past us or into the original accident.

Fires resulted from space heaters, fireplaces, candles or Christmas trees and then when the temperature warmed up, all the frozen, broken pipes let go and we got called to shut off water lines and clean up flooded residences. No wonder I never wanted to rush home and take my kids sledding.

So as I put on another pot of coffee and sit down at my laptop in my cozy office, I will think kind thoughts of those who are getting up early to slide to work or school. Slow down, take your time and look out for each other. May the plow be with you. At least that's what McGregor says.

Jim McGregor

One Second Makes a Difference

I don't know how many of you are aware that we added a 'Leap-Second' to our Atomic Clock last weekend. Specifically, in Langley, the addition occurred at 3:59:60 on December 31st. 2016. We were not required to turn clocks back or ahead, we didn't have to fiddle with our computers or appliances, and this second was apparently added for us.

I checked and everything seems to be ok, my microwave is still flashing 12:00 so there has been no interference in my house. Every now and then a leap second is added to Coordinated Universal Time (UTC) in order to synchronize clocks worldwide with the Earth's ever slowing rotation.

Two components are used to determine UTC (Coordinated Universal Time) :

1. **International Atomic Time** (TAI): A time scale that combines the output of some 200 highly precise atomic clocks worldwide, and provides the exact speed for our clocks to tick.

2. **Universal Time** (UT1), also known as Astronomical Time, refers to the Earth's rotation

around its own axis, which determines the length of a day.

When the difference between UTC and UT1 approaches 0.9 seconds, a leap second is added to UTC and to clocks worldwide. By adding an additional second to the time count, our clocks are effectively stopped for that second to give Earth the opportunity to catch up with atomic time.

The reason we have to add a second now and then is that Earth's rotation around its own axis is gradually slowing down, although very slowly. Well, doesn't that explain a lot? Here I thought it was just me slowing down and being more fatigued but it's the entire earth that is moving slower.

Now I know why it seems to take me longer to get ready in the mornings, why the traffic is moving slower and why people seem to take longer to get the punch lines of my jokes. Our minds and bodies are moving slower.

Some days you feel like you are moving in mud. You keep looking at your watch and the hands don't seem to be moving. You start to think maybe you are suffering from depression or Seasonal Affective Disorder, when now we find out that whole planet has shifted down a gear and has pulled into the intergalactic slow lane.

I used to be able to shovel my driveway in ten minutes, now it takes all morning. I am moving so slow my whiskers seem to be popping up before the second blade gets to them and it now takes me an hour and a half to watch *60 Minutes*.

I used to blame the staff at Tim Horton's for their slow service now I realize that it is taking one second longer to brew the coffee and bake the doughnuts. The baker is not loafing, the oven is taking longer to heat up, and really, waiting one second longer for coffee is not grounds for complaint.

Why wasn't there more publicity about this? No doubt, oil tankers taking one second longer to cross the ocean, is the main reason oil companies are now charging $1.50 a liter for fuel.

I know a lot of you are not reading as fast as you used to, so I typed this as slow as I could. Take your time this year. At least that's what McGregor says.

Will Power for the New Year

The people that know things and research stuff tell us that the majority of us have broken our New Year's resolutions by the last week of January. For many people, the good intentions have waned and they have found out that when they said, "I should do this," they were actually saying, "I have no intentions of doing this." It's the word "should" that creates the problem here and has to be replaced with "I will."

It's not easy. You're driving home and you know you have a Tupperware container in the fridge containing carrots and celery sitting beside a piece of leftover chicken from last night and some nice cold bottles of water. "I should go home and have that for dinner," you say.

But at every red light there is a fast food place that is offering a bacon-covered, double patty burger with a side of fries dripping in grease and salt and a large ice-cold cup of soda pop. It's right there, you should go home, but all you have to do is turn on your signal, go through the drive through and you can have it all eaten before you get home and no one will know the difference, if you haven't spilled anything down the front of your shirt.

My doctor suggested I lose some pounds as one step to reducing my blood pressure. I decided to go about it sensibly and set a goal date of my birthday in March. I said, "I will lose the required amount of weight by the first week of March." I was doing Ok until someone pointed out that next week is February already so, more carrots, less of the stuff that tastes good.

A friend of mine got into trouble at Christmas. His wife had told him she wanted to wake up Christmas morning and see something in the driveway that would go from zero to two hundred in four seconds, so he bought her a bathroom scale. He is still alive but he walks funny now.

I mention that because I needed a new bathroom scale. The one I have was purchased at a garage sale about four years ago. It still has the little bright green, round sticker that says $1. But it is old technology and when you step on it, springs and gears start whirring and the needle on the dial bounces fifty pounds each way before it settles down.

It is hard to read without my glasses and I leave them off because of the added weight. I don't wear rings or a watch either. When you are on a weight loss program, a little swing one way or the other is cause for either elation or depression.

My new scale has a larger platform to stand on, a bright blue digital readout that I can see without bending down, and it has the tenths on it as well which is also encouraging some mornings when you can see the rice cakes you devoured have allowed you to lose one tenth of a pound since yesterday.

It's still early in the year. Re-adjust your thinking, set new goals and start saying 'I will' instead of saying 'I should.' Take over the management of your mind and body and do what is right for you, not what some paid spokesperson on TV says you should do. At least that's what McGregor says

Too Cold for Penguins

I read a rather disconcerting report that officials at the Calgary Zoo recently brought the penguins inside because it was "too cold." If there was ever an indicator of climate change it is penguins asking to come inside and watch TV instead of playing in the snow.

The manager of communications for the zoo, told reporters, "On cold days like this, we have to make that choice for them because it is so cold, but on other days, we do give them the option of coming in and out as they please."

Obviously my parents are not running the Calgary Zoo. When it snowed, we were in or we were out and if we went out we could not plead it was too cold to get back in. The fresh air was good for us and we could not come in and out as we pleased.

Part of the problem is what the penguins are wearing. When they moult they shed everything and grow new feathers and fur. They don't keep anything behind for layering when the temperatures drop.

At the first snowfall my Mom would get us to drag out the winter trunk. This trunk contained woollen snow pants, mittens, toques, scarves and long johns. When you opened it, the stale, musty odour of many winters past came wafting out and took your breath away.

There were no bright nylon jackets or vinyl snow pants and no gaily colored hats or waterproof gloves, just dark, heavy woollen garments. If you had grown over the summer, Mom did not pick up a flyer and see who was having a sale; there was a simpler solution.

Jimmy got Jack's stuff, Gordy got Jim's and Kenny got Gordy's clothes. Jack was in the Air Force so his was all supplied by the government now. This is called Planned Parenthood.

On went the long johns and a pair of woollen socks, then jeans, then snow pants that weighed a ton even before they got wet, and finally a coat that came down to your knees. Top all that off with a scarf, mittens and either a toque or a hat with earflaps and you waddled out into the snow. No wonder my brothers and I never won a snowball fight.

But we had lots of neighbour kids. We built snow forts or snow men and if our wet hands got cold we knew we could not run home crying, we had been taught to shake our hands vigorously, enduring intense pain, until the circulation came back. I wonder if penguins can be trained to do that.

When I finally dragged at least one little brother home on the sled Dad had made from plywood, we were let in and told to hang up our snow clothes. Woollen clothes drying over a heater is a smell that is never forgotten.

Don't be surprised to hear that the lions at the Vancouver Zoo need sunscreen next summer. At least that's what McGregor says.

The Seasons

A local photographer produced a book of photographs and asked me to write a foreword as part of the introduction. As I looked through his amazing collection I felt like I was walking through a calendar.

I hope that the words in this book have given you the same experience and if you happened to call up a long lost memory or two, I would be very pleased. Thanks!

Jim McGregor

Calendar Journey

I've wandered pages in your pathway,
Stopped awhile, here and there;
Stepped into my favorite season
And spent a moment there.

I've leaned on wooden fences,
Watched the early morning sun
Burning holes in autumn hazes,
As the day had just begun.

I smiled quietly in wonder
At each peaceful country scene;
Then heard the bustle of the city
Where the farmland once had been.

I peeked into the window
Of a weathered country church,
Said a prayer for saints and sinners
Then continued on my search.

I spied a totem standing sentinel
Over houseboats time has tossed,
Into an ancient flowing river
Our historic legends crossed.

The Seasons Go Around and Around

Here are fields that I have worked in,
Parks and pools where I have played;
Summer meadows filled with sunshine
Where my love and I have lain.

Like driving through a calendar,
Each page brings its point of view,
The lens captures just a moment,
The memory's up to you.

ALSO BY JIM MCGREGOR

When we sort through our old black and white family photos, scroll down our Facebook pages or thumb through the albums on our phones, we always stop at the memories of Christmas Day, New Year's Eve, the Valentine's, Dance or the Halloween party. The special days of our lives bring together family and friends, in some cases only once a year, and we watch children grow, fashions change, or people come and go from our lives. The stories collected here have been chosen from weekly newspaper columns written over a ten-year period and, while they are pulled from the memories of the author, they will resonate with anyone who has grown up surrounded by family and transport the reader back to a snow-covered road, a country kitchen table, or the memory of that perfect Christmas tree.

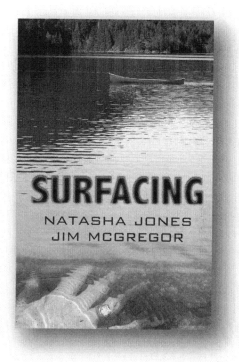

Jeremy knows about the accident but when his mother, Debbie, finally reveals the truth, he has no idea that he will find his once strong firefighter father still unconscious in an extended care facility. The discovery that, after three years, his father suddenly begins regaining consciousness sets in motion a series of events that will rock many lives. Debbie must confront her own challenges, fears and even her ambivalence about her husband's comeback while dealing with her teen-aged daughter's increasing distance and her son Jeremy's mystical behaviour.

Jim McGregor's books are available online in print and e-book.

23812616R00214

Made in the USA
Columbia, SC
17 August 2018